This
Teaching
Life

This
Teaching
Life

HOW I TAUGHT MYSELF TO TEACH

Selma Wassermann

Foreword by Larry Cuban

Teachers College, Columbia University
New York and London

Published by Teachers College Press, 1234 Amsterdam Avenue, New York, NY 10027

Portions of Chapters 1, 7, and 11 reprinted from "Leaving," by S. Wassermann, 2002, *Phi Delta Kappan, 83*, pp. 792–795; from "Quantum Theory, the Uncertainty Principle and the Alchemy of Standardized Testing," by S. Wassermann, 2001, *Phi Delta Kappan, 82*, pp. 28–40; from "Using Cases to Study Teaching," by S. Wassermann, 1994, *Phi Delta Kappan, 75*, pp. 602–611; and from "A Case for Social Studies," by S. Wassermann, 1992, *Phi Delta Kappan, 73*, pp. 792–795. Reprinted by permission of Phi Delta Kappa International. Copyright © 2002, 2001, 1994, and 1992, respectively, by Phi Delta Kappa International.

Portions of Chapters 7 and 8 reprinted from "Learning to Value Error," by S. Wassermann, 1989, *Childhood Education, 65*, pp. 233–234, and from "Aspen Mornings with Sylvia Ashton-Warner," by S. Wassermann, 1972, *Childhood Education, 48*, pp. 348–353. Reprinted by permission of the Association for Childhood Education International, 17904 Georgia Avenue, Suite 215, Olney, MD 20832. Copyright © 1989 and 1972, respectively, by the Association.

Library of Congress Cataloging-in-Publication Data

Wassermann, Selma.
    This teaching life : how I taught myself to teach / Selma Wassermann.
      p. cm.
    Includes bibliographical references and index.
    ISBN 0-8077-4501-4 (cloth : alk. paper) — ISBN 0-8077-4500-6 (pbk. : alk. paper)
    1. Wassermann, Selma. 2. Teachers—United States—Biography. I. Title.

LA2317.W34A3 2004
371.1'0092—dc22
[B]   2004048063

ISBN 0-8077-4500-6 (paper)
ISBN 0-8077-4501-4 (cloth)

Printed on acid-free paper
Manufactured in the United States of America

11 10 09 08 07 06 05 04   8 7 6 5 4 3 2 1

For Jack

Contents

Foreword

The most important day I remember in all of my life is the one in which my teacher . . . came to me. . . . It was the third of March, 1887, three months before I was seven years old.
—Helen Keller

MOST READERS of this book can savor the memory of a teacher who left their signature on their life. Perhaps not the exact day and year as Helen Keller did in remembering Anne Sullivan, but each of our memories holds the truth of a gifted teacher touching a mind and heart forever.

It is especially important now to mark the moment of teacher and student coming together, as did Helen Keller, because the criticism of public schools and teachers that began after World War II continues unrelentingly into the first decade of the 21st century. Many Americans forget in the midst of constant attacks upon public schools that exceptional teachers in and out of classrooms have shaped the lives of kindergartners, teenagers, and college students.

Contributing to the collective amnesia about first-rate teaching is that so few teachers have the time, energy, or inclination to write of their experiences in schools and with children, and their trek from novice to veteran. The conspicuous absence of teachers' voices in talking about their lives in and out of classrooms has constricted public debates about schooling.

Of course, some teachers have written with such candor, humor, and deep truth that their work has entered the canon of teacher autobiographies. Jesse Stuart wrote about his rural schoolmaster days in Kentucky before World War II. Sylvia Ashton Warner wrote about her work in New Zealand classrooms. Bel Kaufman's disguised tale caught high school teaching in New York City schools in the 1950s. Herb Kohl and Jim Herndon captured the tone and texture of teaching poor minority children in the 1960s. And Bill Ayers revealed the difficulties and vulnerabilities of teaching urban youngsters in subsequent decades.

These teacher narratives tell of a passage from inept beginner—teacher education seldom shows up well in autobiographies—to a far wiser veteran who is willing to offer practical advice to those who enter the profession. It is to this canon of teacher autobiographies that I nominate Selma Wassermann's This Teaching Life.

Why? The reasons are many. The graceful and humorous writing invites the reader to turn the page. Wassermann describes her first principal as "one of those perfectly behaved people who never sweat in summer, leak mayonnaise from a tuna fish sandwich, or write a crooked line of print." Going beyond elegant turns of phrasing, Wassermann's narrative, unlike most other teacher accounts, describes the occasional loss of nerve and failed classroom practices. Wassermann devotes a chapter to a sabbatical year in the classroom—yes, she left a university post not to travel or to do research but to teach. She wanted to refresh her knowledge of teaching because she taught undergraduates who were preparing to enter classrooms. That sabbatical year turned out to be especially hard upon her, yet a powerful learning experience—she writes about it for the first time in 30 years—because she learned much from her many stumbles in teaching a difficult group of fifth and sixth graders. As she says elsewhere in the book, "Critical self-scrutiny is not for sissies." And it is this finely tuned reflection on children as whole human beings in classrooms, her strengths and limitations as a teacher, and her stubborn effort to keep getting better that makes this a remarkable tale.

Wassermann's professional journey, however, is more than a well-written account filled with the wisdom of practice for those who want to teach. Interwoven with stories of her classrooms is a zigzag journey of personal growth and how she taught herself to teach through constant reflection on her actions.

To teach, Wassermann reminds all of us, is to live with classroom dilemmas that demand choices daily. And making decisions is what teachers do hundreds of times a day. Wassermann's personal journey reveals how learning who you are helps considerably in coping daily with the uncertainty inherent in classroom decisions. So does converting that self-knowledge, what you know about your children, your subject, and your skills, into something practical that gives students in a classroom a mind-enhancing slice of life rather than a clock-watching exercise. What matters even more for teachers is assessing what happens in classrooms and figuring out better ways to teach next time. All of this self-probing is very tough to do.

So our gifted teacher-writer reminds us that if location, location, location is the central message of buying real estate and practice, practice, practice is how a musician gets to Carnegie Hall, then Selma Wassermann's account of how she taught herself to teach offers those who enter teaching the core lesson of her journey: reflect, reflect, reflect.

Larry Cuban
Stanford University

Preface

THERE IS AN OLD, tired joke in which one man stops another on Fifth Avenue in New York City and asks how to get to Carnegie Hall.

Practice, practice, practice!

So how do you get to be a teacher? Perhaps I might have saved a lot of paper if I had just cut to the chase: Practice, practice, practice! Yet anyone who knows music will know that it takes a great deal more than practice to reach the level of a virtuoso. And anyone who knows teaching will know that it takes a great deal more than spending time in a classroom to become a competent professional.

My story begins with my very humble and inept bumblings as a new teacher and tracks the important steps I've taken in my professional journey toward becoming more competent. In the process of growing and learning, I have shifted perspectives with regard to what I consider important in the act of teaching and in promoting student learning, and I have experienced a sea change in my teaching behavior—from center-stage, deeply traditional "teacher in charge," to student-centered teaching that is light years from my beginnings. And wonder of wonders, after 50-plus years, until I packed up my office and headed out the door to retirement city, my joy in being a teacher never diminished.

In describing the journey of THIS TEACHING LIFE, I hope I've made clear what has "made this teacher"; that teaching is not a profession for the faint hearted; that one dedicates oneself to a lifetime of growing and learning that is challenging, frustrating, but inevitably enriching; that learning brings new perspectives, and new perspectives bring changes to practice. Identifying the pivotal steps along the way, the people whose influence encouraged me to take the risks involved in change, the students who were my best teachers—that is at the heart of the book, and I hope I have done justice to them all.

My professional journey has been enriched by four brilliant teachers—and I count myself incredibly lucky to have had these people touch my life. My dear friend Roland Christensen ("Chris") opened new doors for me in the how and what of case method teaching and urged me again and again to write this book. I am bereft over his untimely death; but he was, nonetheless, "on my shoulder" as I wrote, urging me forward. My main man, Louis Raths, a true educational pioneer, was the first to teach me what teaching could be and was a constant source of inspiration and support in all my professional endeavors. If anyone is to be credited with my understanding of "the art of the question," it is my mentor, "Dudy." Ed Lipinski was my great teacher in clinical work and interpersonal responding. My friend-of-the-heart, Sylvia Ashton-Warner, profoundly influenced my writing and helped me cross the bridge from academic discourse to narrative. All these great teachers taught me not only through their wisdom, but also through their actions. I studied both, and absorbed everything I could.

At my side, throughout our married lives, has been my husband, Jack, who defied tradition and encouraged me to return to teaching, with a small baby at home. "We'll manage," he told me. And we did. He has never been less than my strongest supporter, my ally, my best friend.

It is really impossible to count up the many and diverse ways in which I have learned from my students over the years—and it didn't matter if they were only first graders or members of the elite group of graduate students with whom I was privileged to work. Their generosity of spirit and their loving forgiveness allowed me to risk, to make mistakes, and to carry on. "It's all right, Mrs. Wassermann," I hear Billy Schuey telling me, and I am strangely comforted. I want especially to remember those students from the early days who have sought me out—whether by mail, personal visits, or e-mail messages—to let me know that they still think of our work together as having meaning in their lives. Among many things, these tributes, however overly generous, allow me to believe that, even fumbling and bumbling, I might have managed to do something good.

Appreciations must also go to Rich Chambers, Steve Fukui, and Maureen McAllister for giving me permission to tell stories about their classrooms; Wally Eggert for permission to quote so liberally from our *Profiles of Teaching Competence*; Stefi Wolmer and Robert Leahy, who came to see me and shared with me their memories of being in my class; and Larry Cuban, friend, mentor, and colleague, who graciously consented to write the foreword to this book. Finally, to my superb editor, Susan Liddicoat, my heartfelt thanks for the kind of editorial feedback that keeps my writing in focus and is a model for evaluative feedback anywhere.

There is a long list of others whom I have neglected to mention personally, but they—like all those who have touched my teaching life—are very much in my heart.

①

Leaving

THE PIECE of wood is heavy in my hand and I stand there, unable to decide what to do. Julie Kellog-Smith's name is still clearly visible on the back with the date—this roughly hewn driftwood sculpture with painted clown face, from that Grade 6 class back in 1969. It has traveled with me from office to office, tracking my movements through university corridors, a relic from an archaeological dig into my teaching life. I am marching boldly into retirement, packing up my office, my memories spread out in a lifetime of collected treasures.

The dilemma tears me up—toss it or take it? I cannot bear to give it up, but there's no room in the small apartment where I now live. For the moment, I defer. When in doubt, postpone. I heft the large piece of wood and maneuver it into the packing box. The clown face smiles up at me. Gotcha! I go through the same crisis with each piece: Debbie Jacobi's still life with flute and apple (1960); Bill Renton's wooden leaf carving (1972); Abbey Seiderman's framed oil painting (1969); Frank Wise's photo (1976) of him standing knee deep in the Pacific Ocean with fiddle tucked under his chin—the Spirit of the Delicious Alternative. In the end, I pack them all. They will remain boxed in the underground storage area until my great-grandchildren dig them out. My personal time capsule.

It is surprisingly easy to empty the shelves of graduate students' theses, binders with notes from faculty meetings, folders with workshop materials created for in-service professional development. I donate the theses to the Faculty Associate offices, in the event that they may be useful to anyone who might want to pursue graduate studies. The workshop materials and faculty notes are tossed without

Which to keep? Which to toss?

hesitation. Teresa Saunders wanders into the office as I am studying the academic robes that have served me for 40 years. The black
gown is etched with rust-colored sun stripes that mark the areas
between the folds in years of service. The cap, with gold tassel,
almost new, has been better protected in an overlarge plastic bag
carrying a Brooklyn dry cleaner's label. The light blue velvet trim
on the hood, denoting my field of study—education—is dotted with
water spots from rainy June convocations. Teresa gleefully makes
off with my gown as a souvenir, and thus I avoid another decision.
Would I have had the courage to put it in the trash? I wonder what
on earth she is going to do with it.

From behind the bookshelf I pull several homemade "big books"
—inscribed with messages of appreciation and love from students
who wanted to be remembered. I try to put faces to the names, but
the faces and names of too many other, more recent students have
crowded out any chance for recollection. These yellowed pages have
become messages from strangers. Even so, I sigh as I see these awk-

ward big books, sticking out of the paper-recycling container, re-proaching me for my callousness. I'm trying to be ruthless, keeping the packing lean and mean, but whoever said it would be easy?

In the meanwhile, downstairs in the large, open-area classroom that has been identified with my courses for the past thirty years, the teaching still goes on. Sixty-one students are enrolled this summer in Education 483: Curriculum Studies—Teaching for Thinking, for eight credits, in my last teaching semester at the university. While I know full well that the end of the semester will be THE end, the moment-to-moment sweetness of being with my students and the satisfaction of being their partners in learning does not diminish. I teach this course as if it were my first—although hopefully with some greater skill and wisdom. But the learning about teaching that comes from intimate observation and self-scrutiny goes on unabated. I don't think about where I will now put what I have learned from this group; I don't think about that at all.

"Why do you want to be a teacher?" he asked me when, in my sophomore year, I was applying for entry into the teacher educa-tion program at City College, in New York. Dr. Carter was one of the gray eminences in the School of Education, and he was much feared for his reputation of intimidating students.

"I love children," I answered, thinking how clever I was.

"Well, why don't you marry and have some," he said without humor. He had heard that response before, and it did not persuade him that here was a candidate who was worthy of acceptance.

"I don't plan to marry until I am much older." I faced the lion. "I want to have a career." I stared into those unbelieving eyes. Most of the young women in my peer group were sporting engagement rings, and those who weren't were actively on the lookout for eli-gible young men who would provide them.

Whatever Dr. Carter was looking for in a candidate, his turned-down mouth told me that I did not seem to have the right stuff. He shuffled through the folder containing my application and said, without looking up at me, "You'll have to lose some weight." His words stung me and my throat went dry.

"I will," I told him. "I am already on a diet and will lose twenty pounds by the time the semester begins." All lies, of course. With a stroke of his pen, he admitted me into the program. I left the interview and headed for the subway to Brooklyn, stopping for a candy bar on the way.

Why did I want to become a teacher? While it was true that I loved children and enjoyed spending time with them, becoming a teacher was not, initially, my consuming passion. I had begun my college studies with a business administration major, and found the program lifeless. I longed to be elsewhere—but women in 1946 were considered unacceptable as liberal arts majors; the city's finances would be wasted on their education, for they would inevitably wind up in the kitchen, we were told. I had struck out with business; and engineering, also open to women, was definitely not an option. So

Becoming a teacher was not initially my consuming passion.

while I made noises to the contrary in my interview with Dr. Carter, I was actually coming into teaching by default.

It wasn't until I started my student teaching practicum that I began to feel the exhilaration about teaching that has never left me. The headiness of being with a class of students—I had never felt the like of it. The more I was in it, the more I wanted to be there. Even then, in my professional virginity and hapless naïveté, I knew that it was important to treat children with kindness and respect. Even then, I knew that certain actions I observed in my mentor teacher's behavior were wrong and unhealthy for children's learning and self-esteem. Even though I didn't have the words to express those feelings, I knew in some deep inner place what teaching could, ought, to be.

Miss Stellwagon, my first-grade teacher, was my "first teacher." She taught me about favorites (I was not one) and about talking in class (I was one). She taught me about keeping young children at arm's

Miss Stellwagon taught me about favorites. I was not one.

length, lest their poverty rub off on the teacher's middle-class self. She taught me that discipline meant humiliation and loss of self-esteem, which diminished you. She taught me that even if you tried to please the teacher, unexpressed standards and expectations would kill your chances of being chosen for a part in the play. She taught me that what I enjoyed most (reading) could be made excruciatingly painful, when the same story was read orally, line by line, up one row and down the other, until all meaning and pleasure were extinguished. She taught me that truth had no place in teacher-student interaction; that we were expected to tell her only what she wanted to hear. She taught her slum children "the King's English" and we recited, tongues flicking in and out like frogs', in small hand mirrors, "Jack in the booox, alll shuttt up tighttt; nottt a breath of ayre, nottt a breath of lighttt. How darkkk it musttt beee. He cannottt seee. Open the booox, and uppp jumps heee." She taught us to sit still, without moving, for 3 hours in the morning and 2 in the afternoon, no matter what physical urges came upon you—for to move, or speak, or ask to go to the bathroom would incur a wrath that was terrifying. We waited for spring, for the trees to bloom, for the windows of the classroom to be open, for the end of the term, for the end of Miss Stellwagon.

"And now, boys and girls, I have some very good news for you. Guess who your teacher is going to be next term?"

"Who?" we shouted in excited anticipation.

"I am," she said, her mouth forming into that bird's-beak smile. "Aren't you pleased?"

"Yeesss, Miss Stellwagon," we chanted, our hearts sinking. Two years with Miss Stellwagon left such an imprint that I can remember it still—the smell of the room (chocolate-covered graham cracker cookies mixed with chalk dust), the bleak beige of the unadorned walls with only black-and-white alphabet cards to divert the eye, the steam coming in staccato spurts out of the vent on the radiator, the perfect handwriting on the blackboard, the door with the little window, offering a tantalizing glimpse of the outside, where real life ran counterpart to our still-life experiences. I didn't know it then, but Miss Stellwagon's teaching would be pivotal in my own professional development, my loathing of her so intense that I could only become her antithesis.

Peter comes over to the table where I am sitting, matching the names and photos of the students, studying faces, looking for any clue that will serve as a mental mnemonic to help me remember who is who. This is something that I have to work hard at in this first week of class, and I invent games to fix the name to the face before the seminar begins.

"How *do* you remember all our names?" Peter asks. He will be completing the professional program at the end of the summer and heading into his own teaching life, where he will face 120 secondary school students each teaching day.

"Not easily," I tell him. I wish I could be one of those people who has instant recall and can remember names, places, dates on demand—but that has never been one of my strengths. "I look for facial clues and other identifying features. I'm OK after the third class—that is, if nobody changes their hairstyle and everybody wears the same clothes."

"Oh, I thought you had some kind of magic that you could share with me."

I can remember when I was on my own desperate quest for the "magic" that would make the totality of teaching clear, answer all my questions, prevent all problems from occurring. Peter turns away and my eyes follow the slouch of his shoulders as he goes to rejoin his study group. I have disappointed him. He is looking for a guru and I am only a teacher in my own struggle to learn. But I have long ago stopped wishing that I could give students the magic they will need to solve all their educational problems and right all educational wrongs. I am comfortable with the realization that their struggles are what matters in shaping who they are and what they will become as teachers, that the struggle must be part of each professional journey.

The study groups disperse and come to join the circle for the discussion seminar. The circle is tightly formed, and all students dutifully place their tagboard name cards on the floor so I can see them. I remember all the names at first without looking at the cards, but when the discussion gets more intense, I begin to fumble. I call Kendra Wendy, and I lose Margo's name altogether. Nonetheless, they are pleased that this is important to me and are forgiving of my gaffes. I promise them that I will do better the next day. Of course, the better I get to know them, the more they become real people to me, the easier it is to remember their names. So much for magic.

In the seminar, we are examining principles of inquiry teaching, identified in an article by Gerald Bracey (1998) from an issue of *Phi Delta Kappan*. Their comments about the principles suggest that they are in deep dissonance around the issue of "closure." One of the principles states: "The teacher rarely tells students what he or she thinks they ought to know." I hear the same disclaimers that I have heard lo, these many years:

> But aren't there some things that students *should* know?
> But shouldn't you tell them, at the end of the lesson, what they should have learned?
> But doesn't summarizing the lesson help them to be clear about what they should know?

All statements starting with "But" are a tip-off, for surely what is to come is a protest that real danger lurks in these principles of inquiry teaching for the real world of practice. I wrestle with myself, trying to keep a neutral tone, as I respond with clarifying questions, rather than arguments, trying to keep in mind that this is only the third class, that despite their reasons for signing onto this course, they are still neophytes with respect to theory and classroom applications of inquiry-based teaching. We all have a lot of work to do before they are able to take the first steps away from their deep-rooted programming in "right-answer" modes of teaching and learning.

With each new class, though, I have to teach myself all over again that where we are at the beginning of the semester will be, should be, very different from where we wind up at the end. For isn't that what teaching is about—the expectation that students will, through what they have learned, change in some significant and wonderful ways? Where does my own impatience with this growing and learning process come from?

Returning to the office after class, I am disconcerted by the mess of the boxes, but I feel acutely the need for the dissonance that the boxes bring. I don't want to be lulled into not remembering that my time here is short lived. There *should* be boxes. There *should* be an unsettled air about my life here. I need to be prepared to go.

Art Jonas telephones me from New Jersey. We are old buddies, dating back to doctoral days at New York University. Art teaches at Kean College and says he enjoys his teaching still, and now that the Supreme Court of the United States prohibits enforced retirement based on age, he plans to continue teaching for as long as he remains healthy. I envision him as a wizened old man of 90, beavering away. (Wasn't William Kilpatrick lecturing to large groups of students at Columbia University when he was 80?)

It is different in Canada. At age 65, the university opens its exit door, professors are awarded emeritus status, and booted out. No matter if they are healthy or if their scholarship is robust and significant; no matter if they are excellent teachers or that their students find their teaching of value. The Supreme Court of Canada has upheld the university's right to do this; yet we have important laws against discrimination of all other kinds. I have wrestled with this ruling in my own mind and tried to reconcile myself to the inevitable. Maybe it is important for the "old guard" to make space for new recruits to the faculty. A faculty is, after all, regenerated with new blood and new ideas, and this is a welcome, healthy condition of university life. But I cannot help feeling resentful about not being given a choice. Would I have remained in teaching if it had been possible?

It's hard to pull out the threads of the true feelings—resentment over this discriminatory act of ageism or resentment over the fact of my own seniority. How can it be time for me to pack up my belongings and leave teaching, when I have enough energy to take on another hundred years of classes? What will the days be like from now on, without the excitement and challenges that are such concomitants of a teaching life?

In my dream, I'm visiting Steve Fukui's Grade 11 social studies class. He is teaching a case, and I'm sitting at a desk, among his students, feeling the tension mounting, as he expertly leads the discussion. The feeling of wanting to be *teaching*, of displacing Steve and taking over the class, is palpable, and I wake with a longing that cannot be assuaged.

Growing Professionals

I SPENT A restless night and woke in a sweat. Although I tried to comfort myself by chanting the mantra "Nobody dies from being observed," I was as nervous as a chicken heading for the chopping block. Dressing carefully—I didn't want to lose any points for APPEARANCE—I took the subway uptown and arrived at the school in plenty of time to prepare my teaching materials and make sure the room was tidy.

This was to be my first observation as a student teacher, and I choose the "quick and easy" route, to protect myself from failure. I would read a story to my Grade 1 class and then engage them in a discussion about it afterward. I couldn't go wrong with that plan. Even the more "wiggly" kids loved a good story, and a story would reduce the likelihood of having to deal with "behavior." It never occurred to me that any literate sixth grader could have done the same job, that reading a story was not a way to "show my stuff" and get feedback that would help me to grow. The words *dog and pony show* spring to mind.

Dr. Sloane entered the classroom right on time, and with a wave in my direction, he immediately proceeded to the rear of the room, to sit on the adult chair that had been put there for him. He and I had not met before, and the wave was to be the only personal contact he would make. He sat there, in his gray suit and matching tie, eyeballing the room. Six rows of children, in seats nailed to the floor, already admonished by my mentor teacher to BEHAVE, sat with their eyes on me as I rose to take the class. My throat as dry as a 100-year-old bone, I read as if my life depended on it. The children were attentive, and when we began to talk about the story afterward, they responded with the eagerness of 6-year-olds, offering their ideas. When the "show" was over, Dr. Sloane got up from his chair and, with another wave, left the room. I was not to see or hear from him again, until his second and last visit, a month before the end of my practicum, when we went through the same routine. When my grade for the student-teaching semester was posted, I noted with raised eyebrows a mark of B. I had passed student teaching, finished the teacher education program, and entered the ranks of the profession.

What was it that Dr. Sloane was looking for as he observed what I was doing? I would never know that from him. What did I do incorrectly, or ineptly, that brought a grade of B, and not A? What did I do correctly, or skillfully, that brought a grade of B and not a C? What were the professional skills that suggested competence? What were the skills that I lacked? Astonishing as it seems, and as ashamed as I am to admit it, it took years of growing and learning before I could being to understand the complex and varied professional tasks that make up the whole of what a teacher does when she or he is practicing the art of teaching. It took years for me to appreciate, for example, that there is both art and skill in formulating questions that promote children's thinking about the content and big ideas of a story—that not just any old questions serve an educationally valuable purpose. If you cut your professional teeth believing, as I did, that teaching is telling, what else is there to do but maintain discipline and control, so that students will listen, and learn? What allowed me to make any gains in my teaching competence before then was my ability to observe what other teachers did, pick out what I liked from their bags of tricks, and emulate them. Teacher as mimic.

THE ART OF TEACHING

A dozen years later, elevated in position, but not, alas, in wisdom, to a teaching assistantship in the School of Education at New York University, I was sent to observe a student teacher, Phyllis G., who was having her difficulties with a class of lively sixth graders. It was not hard for me to identify with her feelings of stress over this first observation. Entering the room, I tried my best not to be disruptive, and gave her my wave as I crept to the back and sat on the adult chair that had been left for me.

Phyllis was small and slight and probably weighed less than some of the kids in that class. Maintaining control had been a problem for her, and we had discussed that in the teaching seminar. Now I was to see for myself what she had been able to accomplish under my advisory guidance.

The children, sensing that something important was riding on this visit, did their best for Phyllis. Obviously, they cared about what was going to happen to her and did not want to see her fail. They sat quietly, during what I thought to be the most boring lesson on punctuation in the history of educational practice. When one boy grew tired and irritable and started to act out, he was immediately "shushed" by his seatmate, and they both returned their attention to the lesson, pretending an interest that I thought worth an Academy Award. I had to give Phyllis points, for obviously she had established some rapport with these children—and they were going to give her their full support in the presence of the enemy.

When the lesson was over, Phyllis was in a state of high anxiety. We stepped out into the hall, and I tried to reassure her about her lesson. The children were attentive, I told her. They seem to care about you, I added. This counts for something. We arranged to talk further during the seminar, and I went down to the staff room to talk with the regular classroom teacher.

"How's she doing?" I asked. Getting the perspective of the mentor teacher was important in providing me with a database from which I could make a more complete assessment of Phyllis's classroom teaching skills.

The teacher stiffened her voice into professional falsetto. "Well, she's very willing to learn and very enthusiastic about teaching. Of course, she still is not strong in maintaining control. And that is something she needs to work on."

I left the school with my feelings of uncertainty hovering like storm clouds. Phyllis wanted to become a teacher, but her student-teaching placement had been a real challenge for her. Her lesson was dull and unimaginative. Yet the children were "with her," even so. According to her mentor teacher, and her own self-reports, she had difficulty with discipline and control. How was I to evaluate her overall performance? Was it "good"? Was it good enough? Beyond the more widely used criteria of "control and discipline," whatever else was needed for her to be considered "competent" still eluded me. The standard view of teaching as "telling" and learning as "listening" was still very much entrenched in my thinking. That belief system continued to create the framework within which I operated as a teacher and supervisor of student teachers.

In the years since, I have come to understand that such a view of teaching is as simplistic and shortsighted as saying that Shakespeare is a writer of plays. Once the surface layers of "classroom control" have been peeled back, and one looks beyond the one-dimensional view of "teaching as telling," it is possible to discern the more subtle and multifaceted layers of teaching—a dynamic of strategies, skills, and interactive processes that are as artful and exquisite as the choreography of *Swan Lake*. In order to see the art, however, I needed to know what to look for. I needed to know how to apprehend what makes the complex interactional dynamic work to the benefit of children's learning. Of course, such understanding was a priori to any determination of whether teaching is "good."

THE PROFESSIONAL TASKS OF THE TEACHER

Ask any adult who has been to school about whom they considered a good teacher and you will get a range of responses from "She was strict and didn't let us get away with anything," to "He was a human being to us—not some cardboard figure whose home was in the top drawer of the desk." If some adults consider "strictness" to be a desirable quality and others believe it to be detrimental, if some regard "human qualities" as assets and others consider them to be "soft," how is it possible to make determinations of what is good teaching, with any degree of reliability?

There are problems in asking amateurs, "What's good?" about nearly anything, from a work of art to the items on a restaurant menu. Everyone seems to have an opinion—but that doesn't mean that such opinions are informed or reliable. "I know what I like" is simply not adequate in differentiating a masterpiece from an imitation. There are also problems in asking amateurs about teaching, since former students will have a variety of opinions about quality, not all of them wise. In fact, evaluations from students at the college level about their teachers more often indicate that "easygoing" teachers who tend to give higher grades receive better ratings than those who are more demanding in their standards of student performance. Do students and former students really KNOW which teachers are good? It is likely that some do, while others have distorted perceptions that serve their own vested interests. That is why data coming from students, or former students, cannot be taken as truth.

It wasn't until many years after my initiation into the profession that I began to search beyond the surface of teaching to examine what it was a teacher did—the many professional tasks that, in their dynamic interplay, make up the art of teaching. In this quest, I was prodded by the provocative questions of my doctoral supervisor, who would throw a question like a curve ball, so that once it was hurled, the mind could not thereafter rest. "Do you suppose," he mused, "there are some acts that a teacher performs, that are clearly observable, that one would be able to see, if you knew where and how to look?" At first, I didn't know what he was talking about. But he continued, "You know, there must be some acts that a teacher does that are observable—that we could *look* for, when we say that that teacher is doing a good job. If you were observing a doctor, for example, you could say, 'She washes her hands before going into surgery.' And that would be important. And it would be observable. And I wonder if there are acts that a teacher performs that would be equivalent."

The observability of hand-washing was to become a metaphor in my quest for identifying the professional skills of teachers. These functions would, of course, have to be connected to the sine qua non of classroom work: pupil learning. Once identified, such functions would become the standard by which quality, or "good teaching," could be determined. Little did I know that this was to become a pivotal journey in my own professional development.

DEVELOPING PROFESSIONAL CRITERIA FOR ASSESSING TEACHING PERFORMANCE

Before finding direction, sometimes you have to wander about in the fog for a long time. And it was, I fear, many years down the pike after my well-meaning, but largely incompetent, work with Phyllis that I began the search for a developmental tool that would not only identify the professional tasks of a teacher but also provide relevant criteria for determining whether a student teacher might be judged as professionally competent.

The exercise of coming up with such a tool was in itself an adventure, taking several years. In 1972, a teaching colleague, Wally Eggert and I began by surveying about 100 veteran teachers, asking each of them to list five teaching functions that they believed were absolutely essential in contributing to student learning. This was the merest beginning of the task. After receiving their responses, we edited the list and resubmitted that edited list to the same group of teachers for feedback and comment. After two rounds of editing, we then submitted the new list to other groups, which resulted in further modifications. At the end of the process, we were left with 20 teaching functions, which we then categorized into three groups: teacher as person; the teacher's interactions with students; and the interactive dynamic of classroom life—teacher, students, and curriculum (see Figure 2.1 for the list of functions).

For each item on the list, we developed a short "profile" that described the behavior of highly competent teachers as it would be observed in classroom practice (to compare with "The doctor washes her hands before surgery"). We wanted to be able to use the profiles not only to make summative judgments but also as a developmental tool—a means for providing useful feedback to student teachers at formative stages.

The trouble with creating a mirror through which teaching functions might be observed and assessed was that I, from that moment on, was unable to escape using it to reflect on my own practice. Following the law of unintended consequences, the *Profiles of Teaching Competency* (Wassermann & Eggert, 1976) became *my* mirror, forcing me to take a tough, ongoing look at what I was doing in the act that we call teaching, and offering me guidelines for my own professional growth. Even now, so many years later, they continue to insinuate their way into my reflections on my practice.

More than a set of descriptions that identify teaching functions, the profiles are helpful in pointing to teaching strengths and determining areas of needed growth. They are what connects me to the pathway of continuous professional development.

In the chapters that follow, selected profiles have been used as focal points to highlight the "growing steps" of my professional

Figure 2.1. Highly competent teachers.

TEACHERS AS PERSONS

1. Their behavior is thoughtful.
2. Their behavior is self-initiating.
3. They have a clear idea of what they believe, and their beliefs guide their actions.
4. They are problem solvers.
5. They can put new ideas into practice.
6. They are reliable.
7. They have a positive outlook.
8. They are reflective practitioners.

TEACHERS AND KIDS: INTERACTIONS

9. They prize and care about each individual.
10. They know how to observe, diagnose, and use effective teaching strategies with pupils with behavioral difficulties.
11. They use reflective responses to help pupils think about what they are saying.
12. They promote student thinking.
13. There's a lot of interaction among students in their classes.
14. These teachers are real people to their students.

TEACHERS, KIDS, AND THE "STUFF"—CLASSROOM LIFE

15. They know what they are doing and it makes sense.
16. They are knowledgeable in their fields.
17. They use evaluation to promote learning.
18. Their classrooms are vital, alive, and productive places.
19. Their teaching materials are varied, imaginative, and relevant.
20. They unify their groups.

journey. This organization has allowed me to underscore those teaching behaviors that I believe are essential to the learning and well-being of students, no matter the grade level, and give voice to those experiences that have been key to my growth. It is my sincerest hope that it also serves as a framework for those who are in the process of becoming teachers.

③

Bridging the Gap Between Perceptions and Actions

> In their problem-solving actions, highly competent teachers are able to watch themselves and watch the impact of their actions on the problem situation. This they do nondefensively—with an open attitude that allows for assessing the effect of their actions on the situation. They do not see their actions as ways to solve the problem once and for all. They understand that while others may help them, they are ultimately responsible for educating themselves through this process. For these teachers, teaching is an "examined act," and in their ability to take risks to deal with problems creatively, they elevate teaching to an art.

THE ASSIGNMENT was for us to visit a classroom, gathering data about what we observed about teachers, students, and classroom practice—the real world. We were free to select schools throughout the five boroughs of New York City and to make our own arrangements about the how and when of the visits. We were in the 2nd year of our preservice teacher-training program, and most of us thought it a nifty assignment—a chance to see, at firsthand, what our professors of education meant when they talked about good teaching.

It was nostalgia that took me to the elementary school where I had been a student, and I entered a familiar building redolent with the sights and smells of the past, yet I had a jarring sense that this was now foreign territory. The principal was delighted to welcome me—in those days before all visitors were suspect—and he said he thought I would be happy to visit Mrs. Rudolph's fourth-grade class. I would be bound to see some interesting and innovative ideas being put into practice, the kind of stuff I was learning about in teacher education. He seemed proud of his school and proud that I would choose PS 182 for my observation assignment.

When the 9:00 a.m. bell sounded, I was already in my seat in the back of the classroom, watching Mrs. Rudolph greet her class and take them through the opening exercises of the day: flag salute, song, class news. On the chalkboard was an open grid that was to be filled in with the plan for the day. The children were going to choose activities for each time period. "Wow," I thought to myself, "this is so cool!"

"What do you think we should do at 9:30, boys and girls?" Mrs. Rudolph asked, smiling at the rows of fourth graders.

"Yes, Philip?"

"I think we should go outside, for P.E."

"No, Philip." (A smile, like a grimace) "We can't do that. It's much too early for P.E. Does anyone have another idea?"

"Maybe we could have music?"

"Hmmm, Sonia." (Furrowed brow) "That's an interesting idea, but maybe someone has a better idea."

"I think we should have reading."

"Very good, Iris." (Beaming smile) "We could have reading! That's a great idea."

Mrs. Rudolph wrote READING in the empty slot next to "9:30." She then in similar fashion proceeded to fill in all the other empty slots in the day's schedule, eliciting from the children the kinds of activities she felt belonged in the particular time period of the day. This she called "choosing" time, a modern innovative pedagogy, in which children were given choices about how they wanted their day's activities to be scheduled.

Lacking even the most rudimentary awareness of educational practice, innovative or no, I nonetheless knew that Mrs. Rudolph's strategies were tainted with the weight of manipulation. There was no choice; there was only what the teacher wanted the children to do, disguised under a thin veneer of self-selection. But no one was fooled. Not the children, not the teacher, not me.

In what today would be considered unethical and unprofessional, I wrote up my observation of Mrs. Rudolph's class, coming down hard on her for what I perceived to be the discrepancy between what she was advocating (choice for children) and her classroom practice (coercion and manipulation). Naturally, I got a wonderful mark.

RAW BEGINNINGS

My first 4 years of teaching were filled with an overriding sense of needing to "cover the curriculum." Teacher as teller, children as listeners and obeyers. In the absence of meaningful theoretical grounding, I clung to teachers' manuals, following directions about the how and what of teaching lessons, doing the best I was able, with the few resources I had in my bag of tricks. It was not difficult to follow the instructions in the teachers' guides and bring "basic skill" learning to the students in my classes. I worked hard at preparing for my primary graders worksheets that were "cute" and equally hard at marking them, pointing out errors with red X's, and indicating whether I thought the children's work was "good." In marking the worksheets, I believed with the conviction of the unenlightened that I was being helpful, that children would rejoice in learning where they had blundered. I didn't for a minute consider that such feedback might be hurtful to a child's self-esteem, or how feedback could be worded so that the sting of failure might be reduced.

Much of what I did in those years I would now call "prescription" teaching—it was very much like following the steps in a recipe to make a pudding: measuring the ingredients with precision, beating the eggs to the right consistency, setting the oven at the correct temperature—all to ensure a perfect result. There is no doubt that most of my first graders learned to read, write, and spell. I enriched classroom life with a little art (at least I didn't require them to color in shapes on worksheets, and that is a small consolation) and music. I anguished over children who were unable to perform to first-grade standards, but I had few resources to either understand or deal with their learning difficulties. When I saw student progress and achievement, I simply assumed that this was a consequence of my classroom expertise. Years later I discovered how many children actually do learn to read without formal instruction—as they learn to speak, when given a context rich in oral and written language and a modicum of adult intervention.

Classroom discipline was not an issue in the middle-class suburban school in which I cut my professional teeth. The children were by and large pleasant and submissive, except for the rare one or two who acted out (but who nonetheless responded to admonition). To my shame, I resorted to disciplinary measures to bring behavior into line, measures that today, in retrospect, still embarrass me. Like asking children to put their heads down for a time out. Bleh.

During those first 4 years, there was not a single hour, a single moment, that I had need or cause to look at *self*, to examine, with scrupulous introspection, what it was I was doing. There was no call to do that, no understanding of a need for such self-scrutiny. Teaching

I thought it was my job to control children, to get them to follow my orders, to maintain a sense of smoothness.

was just going through the motions to cover the curriculum. That was all there was to it. If you did that, maintained a sense of control over the children, got them to learn their letters and numbers, that was great! Reflection on action, and on self-in-action, were ideas yet to be born (Schön, 1983), and the need for such self-scrutiny even more remote.

At that time I considered myself to be a good teacher, competent in bringing about learning, and caring and decent in my ways with my students. Because I had no rudder to guide my teaching actions and no need to or resources with which to examine my actions, I was missing the big ideas that later informed my teaching life and that were centered around the questions, What was education for? and What teaching actions was I using that were congruent with my overall goals for the education of my students?

If there is a difference between training and educating, it seems that what I was doing fell decidedly into the training camp—my students were being well trained as lesson learners. But I failed them badly by not teaching them to become autonomous individuals, capable of making their own decisions, of solving problems with a can-do spirit, of developing a palpable zest for learning. And without any inner glance, I was certain that what I was doing was good.

LOOKING AT SELF

As I write these paragraphs today, I search back in my memory to see if I can identify that pivotal moment when "looking at self" in the act of teaching became a full-time endeavor in my teaching life. Obviously, there had to be some a priori identification of the need for such a look, some knowledge that bringing perceived self into congruence with real self was a necessary condition not only to good teaching but to all satisfying human interactions.

Without doubt, the building blocks for such professional growth were set in place by the quest for a professional tool to assess student-teaching competence, which I described in Chapter 2. That, however, came long after my immersion in the "personal growth" literature that flooded the market in the 1960s, when life was consumed with the search for inner awareness. The 60s were a time of defiance of authority, a time of pushing at boundaries both outward and inward. Sexual barriers that had dictated moral standards for centuries were being scorned and broken, and psychedelic drugs were "expanding inner horizons." It was a wild time, a time of social and sociological upheaval that made the over-30 generation shudder in horror.

Into the 60s came a flood of books, each advocating its own route to personal fulfillment, and I choose reading, rather than psychedelics, in my own search for inner meaning: Carl Rogers's, *On Becoming a Person* (1961), Fritz Perls's, *In and Out the Garbage Pail* (1969), Robert Lindner's, *The Fifty-Minute Hour* (1954), Thomas Harris's, *I'm OK, You're OK* (1967). These and others in the genre gave me entry into the world of human behavior and provided me with rudiments of understanding of what makes people behave as they do. Where did THAT need come from?

If it had not been the Age of Aquarius, would I have taken these steps? Who knows? But there is no doubt that these books opened doors to wider reading in the field of human behavior and to the more serious clinical literature in psychology, counseling, and therapeutic practice. Inevitably, these texts took me into worlds of human growth and development and taught me much about the growth of a self. It is interesting to note that "personal growth literature" has burgeoned in the past 30 years and is now a cottage industry not only for helping professionals but also for a wider population seeking ways of understanding "who we are and what makes us tick."

NONDEFENSIVE SELF-SCRUTINY IS NOT FOR SISSIES

During the decade of the 60s, a new awareness was emerging about the interactive dynamic of classroom life. One of the pioneers in this field was Ned Flanders (1970), who was the first to begin a systematic study of the transactions between teacher and students and their meaning for student learning. From Flanders's work other systems grew; what they gave educators was the beginning of an understanding that teacher talk—the what and the how, and the student responses that such talk elicited—had great significance for student learning (Parsons, 1971). While these systems proved unwieldy for extended practical use, for me, they laid down another building block in the examination of classroom discourse.

At the same time, a new and intrusive piece of technical equipment entered the lives of teachers-in-training: the videotape recorder. With a video recorder, we were able to look at ourselves and, most especially, at the ways in which we interacted with students. Here again, if interactions were an important key to effective student learning, video playback gave us the means of examining teacher-student interactions in clear, unambiguous ways. In videotape playback, you just couldn't hide from the truth.

Thinking myself wonderful in every way, I invited the videotape recording machine into my classroom and allowed doctoral students from the University of California Graduate School of Education, who were studying classroom questions in relation to pupil thinking, to videotape my lessons with my Grade 5/6 class.

Perhaps in his or her heart, every teacher does believe that what she or he is doing in the classroom is of benefit to student thinking. Of course! Isn't that what education is all about? Don't all teachers want their students to think? I had already embraced this educational goal, and I believed, in my heart, that what I was doing in both my curriculum work and in my discussion strategies was exemplary in carrying out that goal.

It was a hard fall to reality. Until seeing myself on tape, I had no clear vision of the ways in which my questions (now termed *leading*) worked to persuade my students to follow my lead in arriving at the specific answer I was looking for. Far from engaging in open inquiry, I manipulated and subtly directed them to where I wanted them to go. How different was I from Mrs. Rudolph?

There's nothing quite like seeing yourself for the first time in the harsh light of reality. First you cry. Then you can choose one of several pathways. Denial is a wonderful strategy, but it is ultimately ineffective in helping you bring your teaching behavior into line with your educational goals. Avoidance is another technique—"I'll deal with it tomorrow." Takes you off the hook, but only for the moment. What's wrong is still wrong. Rationalization doesn't work either. "I'm not really *like* that! I was just having a bad day" doesn't put you on the road to reform.

To open oneself to critical self-scrutiny is not for sissies. It's much easier to deny, to avoid, to rationalize—but those are not the steps to professional growth. It is VERY hard to accept one's faults, one's shortcomings, one's warts, and to begin there to work on change. No one likes to admit to flaws, and especially so in these modern times, when shirking fault has become a national obsession. But it's the only road to change. Nobody ever said it was going to be easy.

The hard looks I began to take at my teaching actions opened up a world of examining and developing skill in the interactive discourse of classroom dialogue. But the first step, that mean-spirited, rotten, take-a-look-at-self step, I know now, was the only possible starting place.

LISTENING TO SELF IN THE ACT OF SPEAKING

It wasn't the only time I had to face reality in examining the difference between what I was saying to students and what I *thought* I was saying. But the first step put me on the path of studying my interactions and learning to listen as I spoke—reflection-in-action, a burdensome habit from which I was unable to retreat. Such a professional commitment meant taking responsibility for every utterance that came out of my mouth. It meant listening to every word I spoke to others. It meant carrying the burden of owning my statements, and it meant learning to observe and apprehend how my statements affect others, discerning whether they are effective in producing the desired learning results. It also required knowing something about the interactions that are helpful in promoting pupil thinking and learning and those that are counterproductive to pupil thinking and learning.

For these professional skills, which I continue to study and learn, since human interactions do not cease when we stop teaching, I owe a big debt to the therapeutic community and the works of Robert Carkhuff, Bernie Berenson, and Charles Truax, whose research in clinical settings gave rise to understanding how a therapist's interactions were helpful or harmful in helping relationships (Carkhuff, 1969; Carkhuff & Berenson, 1976; Carkhuff & Truax, 1967). From their work I was able to extrapolate my own systems of helpful and harmful classroom interactions and, further, to devise a means of systematic examination of those questions and responses that work to promote pupil thinking (Raths, Wassermann, Jonas, & Rothstein, 1986). To be able to attend to what a student is saying, to find just the right question or response, to know how to phrase it so that it comes out at its most effective, to discern its effect on the student, to hear the student's subsequent response and use that in framing the following question/response—all that, done in milliseconds during an interactive dialogue, has taken a great deal of growing time. But the journey has been more than worth the years of practice, for I believe that these skills are the core of my teaching strength (Adler & Towne, 2002; Brammer, 1993; Gazda, Asbury, Balzer, & Childers, 1991; Hamachek, 1997; Moursund, 1993).

INTERACTION SKILLS PAY OFF

As part of an extensive school renewal program in south Seattle, I was invited to work with a Grade 12 class to solicit their views about what needed to change in their school. The students who had been "volunteered" to participate seemed to me to be largely disinterested in the exercise. They had "been there, done that" with little result in the past. Why should this be any different? As I faced them from the front of the classroom, at least two of them had their backs turned to me; several were glancing at reading material that was hidden under their tabletops; others were engaged in private conversations.

Trying not to show how nervous I was, I introduced myself by telling them that I was a teacher who was very interested in teaching for thinking and wondered if anyone in this class could make any comments about how teaching for thinking was being carried out in their classes. This I did in about 25 words, and then I just waited.

At first there was a great silence, as heavy as a piece of cement block. I waited for what felt an unendurably long time. If the silence was uncomfortable for me, it was at least equally so for the students. Finally, one student broke the deadlock and said that he didn't think there was much concern for thinking in that school and that, in fact, the opposite was true—students were being denied the chance to think their own ideas.

Thus began an inquiry into the lives of students at that school. To some student statements, I offered a reflective response, one that acknowledged and appreciated the contribution to the discussion. To other statements, I raised questions that sought to clarify an idea, an issue, or a position taken. I used attending skills to discern not only what was being said, but also what emotions were shown on faces, and I responded to these cautiously. Throughout all of it, I maintained a neutral stance, not betraying any of my own feelings or thoughts about what was being said. For such skills, I had worked years, spending countless hours studying my own interactions with students on videotape.

Students who had their backs facing the rear of the room turned to look forward and engage in the discussion. Students who had been reading or having private discussions also became participants. I took risks and walked close to the student speakers, as if they and I were in an intimate pas de deux in which their ideas became the most important words that were going to be said that week. Little by little, the students began to reveal all their pent-up anger about their treatment by certain teachers—disrespectful, hurtful, disempowering—and the extent to which they felt cheated by their school experiences.

The principal came to stand at the back of the room, listening but not intruding. The students were not intimidated by her presence—perhaps they felt they were finally getting to say what they wanted her to hear. At long last, she respectfully intervened, to say that I was to be taken elsewhere, and she was sorry to have to bring the discussion to a close. One girl said, "You can't do that! We've only JUST BEGUN to tell what we think!"

It was an important lesson that I learned from this group of students—the power of interpersonal skills to provide a forum in which students could speak their minds, to take risks, to make statements that would furnish a basis for making change in that school. I confirmed, too, the value of listening, attending, reflecting, questioning, and respecting students' ideas as perhaps the most important tool I owned as a teacher, grateful and humbled for the building blocks that brought me to those skills. Finally, I was making some headway in narrowing the gap between my perceptions and my actions.

Putting New Ideas into Practice

Highly competent teachers can take new ideas and put them into practice. They are able to make assessments of group needs, come up with an idea that is appropriate to those needs, and create a scheme for implementing the idea. They are not thwarted by limited resources; they seem to be able to do a lot with a little. They generate excitement about what they are doing. What they do is new and fresh, and there is a sense of life and vitality in their work.

A BBEY LANE SCHOOL, in burgeoning School District 5, was suffering from the rapid-growth pressures of the whole geographical area of Nassau County, Long Island, New York, in the early 1950s. Young families were moving from the cities into the suburbs, and Mr. Levitt was making it possible for the newly married, with children, to afford small, single-family houses, if fathers were willing to make the commute—a one-hour drive each way—into the city to their jobs. Eighty thousand families were easily persuaded that Levittown offered the idyllic life, shelled out modest down payments, and set about establishing a community among what had previously been tilled potato fields. Schools sprouted like spring wheat to accommodate the booming babies, and the strain on the taxpayers' budgets allocated to building new schools was always a source of intense and heated political debate at school board meetings.

To accommodate the rapidly increasing numbers of children in buildings designed for half the actually existing school-age population, the school schedules were created in double shifts—morning and afternoon classes of instructionally intense 4-hour sessions, so that two classes could share the same space. Morning sessions began at 8:00 a.m. and ended at noon. The afternoon classes began at 12:00 p.m. and continued until 4:00 p.m. Double-occupancy classrooms were standard for Grades 1, 2, and 3 throughout the district. But beginning in Grade 4, teachers and children got their own classrooms, following traditional school schedules: 9:00 a.m.–3:00 p.m. Primary teachers shared rooms, cupboards, bulletin boards, and other resources, and we learned to do the "primary shuffle" as the morning teachers quickly moved their children and themselves out of the way of the incoming afternoon groups. If the teachers sharing a single room were philosophically compatible, the logistics of sharing were undertaken cheerfully and accommodations to one another's space were graciously respected. If not, tensions about invasions of space and logistics could easily turn colleagues into adversaries. I chose the morning session, since the prospect of working with young children until 4 o'clock in the afternoon did not appeal to me. At noon, I was finished teaching for the day; joined my colleagues for lunch; and spent the "preparation hour," from 1:00 to 2:00 p.m., working on materials for the next day: writing lesson plans, reading children's work, talking to parents, and doing the thousand jobs that are part and parcel of a teaching life.

After 4 years in Grade 1 at Abbey Lane, I moved to Grade 3—a new adventure for me. I knew enough about organizing a classroom for instruction and quickly learned the Grade 3 curriculum protocols that had been established by the state Department of Education and by local school board mandate. The basal readers and social studies and science texts were several levels higher than for Grade 1, and the concepts to be taught, more challenging. I thought it was going to be great fun to involve my more "mature" students in project work in social studies and to plan trips that went beyond the dairy farm and the petting zoo. I was already beginning to push the edges of the envelope, learning to relax the velvet glove, starting to unload the professional falsetto voice, and becoming more genuine with the children. This seemed to be a reflection of my increased feeling of competence; I was not so uptight about classroom control. Luckily, it was a wonderful group of children who were immensely generous in allowing me to take some big steps toward opening up the curriculum.

Robert Leahy, whom I remembered as a towheaded 8-year-old in that class, with hair that looked like the end of a bristle brush, came to visit me many years later. Now an associate professor at Stetson University in Florida, he was eager to answer my question about what made that class memorable for him.

"That's easy," he said. "You took us on about a dozen field trips, many of them to the city." ("The city" was what everybody called Manhattan—a 35-mile trip from the school.) "My parents didn't have the time or the inclination to take our family to New York on weekends; so going with the class was a wonderful, exciting event for me. And the places we went were thrilling for us. You also invited all of us to your house. I thought that was very cool."

Oddly enough, it was not those trips that made that class memorable for me; nor could Bobby (Robert, excuse me!) have observed the slow process of change that had begun to creep into my teaching practices, making the second half of the school term significantly different for me from the first. As I look back through the distorted windows of memory, I see that four key events were instrumental in altering not only the *way* I taught but, more important, how I *perceived* teaching in that year.

MEETING INDIVIDUAL LEARNING NEEDS— FROM THEORY TO PRACTICE . . . HELP!

First, I began to release myself from the blinders of organizing reading instruction around three reading groups, which had allowed me to ignore children whose own pace did not match the level of instruction for each group. I would love to know what key turned in the lock and opened the door to my apprehension of these children at the outer edges of the reading groups—and why then, and not earlier? In retrospect, it seems that some mysterious combination of factors, taken together, built a "readiness" in me to look beyond accepted practice and discern the fuller picture of what was happening. Whatever was the key, here was a turning point that was to create a sea change in perception and action.

In life we grow accustomed to doing things a certain way, without stopping to reflect on the how or the what. These movements become programmed into us, and we carry out the movements like automatons, in mindless adherence to the program. I imagine that this is what happens while brushing our teeth, or feeding the cat, or making the tea. There are activities that we have learned to do, and do well, without deep analysis. For to analyze everything we do would seem to be a colossal waste of time and surely an impediment to getting anything done.

Children suffer, however, if acts of teaching are carried out mindlessly, in rote application. Because classroom conditions change from moment to moment, teaching requires apprehension of those changing conditions and teacher responses that attend to them. Teaching is the least boring of any job, but apprehending and responding to continually changing conditions is exhausting. It is understandable that teachers might wish to retreat to less arduous and more automatic movements.

Having finally come to the place where I could no longer ignore the instructional needs of children at the outer edges of my three reading groups, I responded by creating additional groups to accommodate those individual needs. My three groups became four, then five. But even this was not adequate. In the end, like the old woman in the shoe, I had so many reading groups that reading became the be-all and end-all of the day's activities. Here I was, finally, finally, having gotten to the point of understanding Dr. Haithcock's advice, when in sophomore year of college she admonished all of us to MEET INDIVIDUAL LEARNING NEEDS! and I was struck down by the logistics. A nice theory, eh? But fails in the application!

BEGINNING GRADUATE STUDIES:
SEARCHING FOR ANSWERS

A second event was my enrollment in a master's program at City College, New York, where I had completed my undergraduate degree. (Was it John Dewey who wrote, "We grow to love our chains"?) During the dry spell of uninspired teaching that made up most of the courses in the program, I was recommended to the remarkable course Diagnosis and Remediation of Reading Disabilities, taught by Professor Florence Roswell, a specialist in the field and the co-author of the Roswell-Chall Diagnostic Reading Test (Roswell & Chall, 1976). This was the first course I had ever taken that combined sound learning theory with classroom application. Classes with lectures were followed by a laboratory, in which each of us was assigned to tutor a child with a reading disability who had been referred to the City College Reading Clinic. In the laboratory, we applied knowledge from our course to undertake diagnosis, plan a program of teaching, and carry out remedial instruction. Regular conferences with a clinic instructor about our laboratory assignments afforded critical assessment of what we were doing, provided insightful feedback, and were the source of helpful suggestions about specific teaching strategies. The textbook was a treasure house of information, expertly presented and elegantly written—an actual tool for advancing my learning. I fell in love with diagnosis and remediation of reading disability. For the first time in my education coursework, knowledge, combined with instruction in *how to,* followed by *application* with feedback, provided me with essential understanding and skills that enabled me to work more effectively with students having trouble with reading. The surge in my confidence to do this work was empowering.

INTRODUCTION TO CHILD-CENTERED TEACHING— WHERE HAVE YOU BEEN ALL MY LIFE?

A third event that occurred that year was a professional workshop for teachers, in which Dr. Jeannette Veatch came to present her pioneering work in "individualized reading" (Veatch, 1966). A demonstration lesson was arranged for primary teachers to observe, and I watched teacher and class, in what was for me the equivalent of hearing the first performance of Stravinsky's *Rites of Spring.* Children selecting their own books, from about 100 library books; reading because they were interested in the material, not because they were forced to read; books that contained real stories that were part of the children's literature collection; instruction that occurred individually, in one-on-one conferences; and phonic skills taught in groups formed around specific skill needs. It was a revelation! And what I wanted to do was to learn more about how this worked. I found that on another professional day, I could visit the Little Red Schoolhouse, in downtown New York City, a private school for the children of the bohemian intellectuals in Greenwich Village, where I could see individualized reading carried out in all the grades.

Between Veatch's workshop and my visit to the school, I read everything I could get my hands on about individualized reading, most materials at that time, in in-house duplicated form, coming from the New York City Board of Education, where May Lazar was single-handedly trying to shift the entire New York City school system into a less rigid, more humanistic, child-oriented reading program. (It didn't work.) With a few colleagues from my school, we drove into the city and spent the day visiting classes at Little Red.

At this hothouse private school, I went wide-eyed from room to room, taking in what was going on. First, the very relaxed way that teachers interacted with students was a source of great amazement. Children called teachers by their first names. By THEIR FIRST NAMES! Girls were allowed to wear pants to school (unheard of in the mid-50s), and in fact, the dress code for teachers and students was very informal. There were no grade designations; children were grouped according to age, so there were the "6s" and the "7s" and the "8s," all the way through to the "11s." Working with art and music was basic to the curriculum; and even the "5s" worked in the wood shop, under the instruction of a specialist teacher. No one was afraid to let even the young children hammer or use the saw or carve—activities that would have caused the principal at Abbey Lane a complete nervous breakdown had she ever learned that children were using such "dangerous tools" in her school. At Little Red, children turned out serious wood projects—and some of the work was masterful.

Every class had music scheduled several times a week, in a program run by Charity Bailey. Music consisted of the children singing pieces selected from a rich heritage of folk songs and learning to play instruments. It also included folk dancing. In one class, the children quietly took off their shoes and socks and danced a Greek circle dance. Boys and girls; no self-consciousness. I had come to see individualized reading in action, and I got a lot more than I had expected—a minieducation in child-centered education. The ideas and practices that I observed excited me as I had not been at any other time in my teaching life so far. I couldn't wait to return to

Abbey Lane School and try some of these activities with my own class.

Being more enthusiastic than thoughtful, I brought in a folk record and, the next day, asked my Grade 3 children to push all the tables and chairs to the sides of the room and remove their shoes and socks for dancing. What an uproar! It was as if I had asked them to remove their undergarments and parade around naked. I heard a litany of complaints, from "My feet are dirty" and "His feet are smelly" to "This is weird." But children are generous and forgiving, and they allowed me, after the initial wild confusion that accompanies a new and very different activity, to instruct them in the steps of the dance. By the end, they liked it and wanted more. It was noisy and a little wild, but I was not worried by the noise and the carefree abandon of the children doing a Greek dance. This was definitely a first step for me; I was learning my own dance.

In another breach of my lockstep way of teaching, we planned and carried out a whole-class mural, using a cut-and-paste medium, of the geographical area around our school. Geography was combined with art—the children worked on the floor, away from their desks. I allowed the noise and the higher energy activity that seemed appropriate for what I had planned. As the mural took shape, I recognized what the children could do, and I felt an affirmation that this, too, was learning.

BREAKING THE CHAINS

I now felt ready to begin extinguishing all trace of reading groups and to go forward with my plan to bring in 100 library books and orient my class to individualized reading. I had watched and studied and read; my questions about implementation had been answered to my satisfaction. I had seen children's enthusiasm for books and reading, and I was motivated. My case prepared, I hustled off to the principal's office to let her know about my plans and my deviation from accepted reading practice.

Una Melton was one of those perfectly behaved people who never sweat in summer, leak mayonnaise from a tuna fish sandwich, or write a crooked line of print. She liked things in order, and she liked to keep her hands on what was happening in every classroom of *her* school. It didn't occur to me, in those days, that her need for control was infantilizing her teachers and strangling every creative force. While we mocked her for distributing supplies from the school storeroom with a specificity that was mind-numbing (for example, issuing 6 inches of masking tape at a time), we did not question her authority to read every comment on a report card before it was sent home, nor to criticize what we had written and ask for changes to be made. We thought it was only tiresome that she would need to read aloud to her faculty long directives from the school board offices, rather than just posting the notices up on the teachers' bulletin board. Mrs. Melton liked the lines of children in the corridor to be absolutely straight; the noise of passing classes in the hallway restricted to shuffling feet; the children clean, courteous, and calm; the teachers following, to the letter, her dictates about the what and how of teaching.

It was not unexpected that a reading program that allowed children to select their own books and read at their own pace would be anathema to this highly controlling administrator. In spite of my careful presentation and my high motivation for beginning this new program, Una Melton dismissed it with a wave of her hand. She looked at me as if I had just dropped my ice cream cone on her clean white blouse.

"Oh, Mrs. Wassermann," she said with a sweet smile that communicated her sadness at my outrageous behavior, "we NEVER do experimental programs at Abbey Lane. Here, we only use the tried-and-proven reading programs. It would be impossible for me to give you permission to do what you are asking."

I left the principal's office feeling, for the first time, trapped by Una Melton's stranglehold on my teaching. I felt her sucking the life-blood from my feelings of personal power. Frustrated and disappointed, I kept the reading groups largely intact, but did allow for children who had finished the third-grade basal reader to move on to library books that they themselves had selected, conferencing with them, individually—despite the refusals of my administrator to sanction these actions. The small inroads I made with individualized reading, behind the back of Una Melton, gave me some grounding in the *how to*, even though my program was marginalized and included only a small group of children. In those last few months before the year was over, I knew that Abbey Lane was already part of my history and that I needed to move out of the box inside which I had allowed myself to be locked.

So what made those sea changes in my own thinking and teaching behavior possible? How come the visit to the Little Red Schoolhouse brought such a charge of excitement? Why did I WANT to be that kind of teacher now? Why didn't I just tell myself that this was education that could only be done in a private school and would not work in a public school setting? It's really impossible for me to say with any certainty, but it is clear that, by then, certain building blocks were already in place, and these new learning experiences seemed to fit with my cognitive field map, so that they now formed a new whole, a new way of looking at what teaching could be and what I could do in my teaching practices. Little did I know that such changes were only the merest beginnings of what was to come, about the equivalent of learning to play the C-major scale with the Beethoven *Apassionata* Sonata in my future.

⑤

Finding Ways to Attend to Individual Learning Needs

Highly competent teachers can make informed, intelligent observations of pupil behavior and use these as data to make diagnoses of problems that interfere with pupil learning. The diagnoses are then used to plan teaching strategies that are appropriate to the individual learner. The observations are free from personal bias and value judgments. They do not label, condemn, attribute, or judge harshly. If a pupil needs special help, she or he is referred to the appropriate agency. While competent to act, these teachers recognize the limits of their own ability.

W HEN THE ADVERTISEMENT appeared in the school district newsletter for an opening for a reading teacher at the new Lee Road School, I was ambivalent about making an application. The thought of leaving the classroom, with its broad spectrum of activities, and which I was enjoying more and more, was not appealing. Yet, yet, yet . . . the possibility of putting my enthusiasm for reading diagnosis, remediation, and individualization into practice in a new setting, free from the shackles of Una Melton, was seductive.

Frank Fusco, the newly assigned principal of Lee Road School, interviewed me at length. I told him about my studies at the reading clinic at City College and of my interest in individualized reading and what I thought such a program could bring to children's attitudes toward reading. I also confessed my reluctance about leaving classroom teaching and bluntly stated that I could forsee that I would miss the classroom so much that I might not wish to permanently remain in the new assignment, if I got it.

The 1950s was a decade of strong social, educational, and cultural conservatism, a quiescent time before the turbulent 60s, which brought the Vietnam War, the civil rights movement, Women's Liberation. But Frank Fusco definitely marched to a different drummer. Not only was he open to innovation, he prized it. Whatever I had said had impressed him enough for him to give me the job. And in September 1956, 300 students and 16 teachers moved into a Quonset hut that had been cobbled together on a piece of land adjoining Southern State Parkway, a temporary building for us to occupy while we were waiting for the new school to be finished. A screened-off section of the gymnasium area was set aside for four "offices" for the special teachers, those providing physical education, music, art, and remedial reading services. The teachers' lounge was in the furnace room. We worked to the background noise of balls thumping on the gym floor and drank coffee tinged by the smell of diesel fuel. Under today's teacher union demands for teachers' rights and prerogatives, this kind of situation would be intolerable. Yet for us the ambiance was delightfully liberating.

In setting up a program for children who were having difficulty with reading, I selected a group from the recommendations of classroom teachers and used diagnostic assessment tools to determine the nature and extent of each child's difficulty. I ordered books of the "high interest, controlled vocabulary" type that were central to remedial programs. Having the clinic experience behind me, and having taken further courses with Professors Roswell and Chall, I was convinced that I *knew* what I was doing and could, through the use of my wonderful skills, teach children, hitherto unsuccessful, to read.

Frank Fusco was my first contact with an educational administrator who seemed to be doing more than sitting in his office counting paper clips and fielding calls from irate parents. Actively encouraging and supportive of teachers' efforts, he also provided thoughtful feedback, which often gave me new insights into my own work. This he did with kindness and with what appeared to considerable understanding of the work I was attempting. With his approval and support, I offered classroom teachers help in setting up individualized reading programs for those who wanted to move in those new directions. I shudder to think of it now. There I was, with the most minimal experience in carrying out individualized reading practices, already teaching others how. My grandmother would have called it colossal chutzpah.

To be able to work collegially with teachers in an encouraging and facilitative environment and to be able to carry out work helping children in acute need nourished me and extended me in many ways. Despite our meager physical accommodations, school spirit was high. When the school building was finally ready the following September, we moved into our new "digs" convinced that we were the best school in the district and had the most going for us. Frank's administration did not infantalize us; it counted on us to perform as professionals.

Of the now 26 members of faculty, the one who opened my eyes to problem-based teaching was Ruth Varon. Ruthie had come late into the teaching profession. She was what was referred to as a "90-day wonder"—a "mature student" who had taken a very short emergency course in teacher education on top of an old degree, so that she, along with others like her, could fill the many teacher vacancies in New York State. Brand new to the classroom, with a heart open to creativity and innovation, she embraced individualized reading as though it was her child. When I watched her work and saw how she had opened other parts of her program to projects and problem-based learning, I was dazzled. Ruth was a beacon in the school, and other teachers soon followed her example, albeit more timidly, on the individualized reading pathway. It was exciting for me to see this work flourish, and I was glad to be able to support her. However, in truth, it was I who was learning more about individualized reading—from "helping" Ruth. I don't think she ever really appreciated that *she* was really *my* teacher in this process. It was she who came up with those brilliant ideas for language-related projects that would flow from the children's reading. It was she who generated a steady flow of curriculum ideas that were never found in any academic textbook. Her classroom was a hive of activity—always messy, always alive, always exciting. Some are born to teach; Ruthie was a natural. Although she would never shirk from letting her kids know when their behavior was "out of line," she was impressive in her ability to relinquish control and allow her pupils their choices in grand, far-reaching ways.

Meanwhile, in my new office on the second floor of the school, with a view out over the trees, I maintained a program of working with children who had reading problems. I quickly discovered that despite all my preparation, my work at the reading clinic, my confidence that certain teaching strategies would inevitably ensure success for my students, some children were just unable to make any meaningful gains. And no matter how I tried, I could not find ways to help them cross the bridge into reading success. Once again, I considered these children my personal failures.

DIAGNOSING LEARNING DIFFICULTIES— ELUSIVE AND MYSTERIOUS PROCESSES

Now I understand more fully that tools and specific teaching strategies go only so far in remediating a student's learning problems. Tests that determine reading levels and skill needs are helpful; gathering background information is helpful as well. Tests of vision and of handedness were also part of the battery of diagnostic procedures I had learned at the reading clinic. They all combined to create diagnostic profiles of students' abilities, and from this I was to make determinations of courses of remedial action. I took all this very seriously.

Giving more credibility to the diagnostic tools than they deserved, I painstakingly recorded formative and summative information about the results and about each student's performance at each instructional session. In retrospect, I see this more as a legitimization of the process than as actually helpful to students.

What did I learn from all this data gathering? In the end, it all added up to the same profile: This student was unable to "perform" at grade level with respect to reading. In too many instances, the reasons continued to elude me, the difficulties seeming to come from some mysterious source, yet to be identified. I thought if I could only figure it out, if I could only find the root of the problem, I would be able to address it and fix it.

In nearly all cases, there was no evidence that the children's teachers had failed them in the teaching of "reading skills." These had been taught, with dedication and concern—but not learned. I knew from my reading and discussions at the reading clinic that "psychological problems" were a serious causative factor in reading disability—but then what? With two psychologists for the entire school district, the likelihood of getting individual attention for a student in difficulty was remote, at best. In those days, a referral to an outside agency was a matter of shame and, unless a student was presenting some very badly disturbed behavior, a highly unlikely possibility. Even with such treatment available, would that have been the key to open the doors to learning?

It wasn't until many years, many experiences, later, that I learned about "fear" of reading—like "fear of flying"—finding that some children, for whatever reason, were terrified of performing in this particular curriculum area, that some children felt so disempowered that they were afraid to try. It wasn't until years and years later that we in the profession began to understand more about the nature and complexity of learning disabilities and the physiological and psychological sources that feed them. Thanks to systematic research in the field, we now know much more about the vast range of disabilities that afflict children and hamper their ability to learn (Feldman, 2002). However, in spite of what we know (Amazon.com lists nearly 24,000 titles under the category "learning disabilities"), when push comes to shove, it is still the classroom teacher who must face the student with singular learning needs and address them in a classroom context, so that a child might take the next steps in learning. To me, this is one of the most daunting tasks of the teacher. During those early years, however, I continued to invest time in further study in my quest to find the keys to these mysteries of life and learning.

BEHAVIORS SYMPTOMATIC OF LEARNING PROBLEMS

"You've got to take a course with Louis Raths," Phil Cardina, a fellow graduate student, advised me. Phil made it sound like an experience not to be missed, and although I couldn't see how Evaluation in Education was going to help me deal with the problems of students with learning disabilities, I nonetheless took his advice. During that hot, steamy summer semester, I found myself sitting in a long, narrow room packed to the walls with rows of tablet armchairs,

"You've got to take a course with Louis Raths!"

3 mornings a week, in 2-hour sessions, for 6 weeks. My initial concern was how to keep my armpits dry in a sweatbox with two small windows and no air conditioning. There must have been more than 80 people in that room, which spoke of the wide and distinguished reputation of this teacher.

It would not be an exaggeration to say that it took about five words from Raths to thrill me with the power of this remarkable teacher. He did not sit, but instead walked back and forth across the front of the room, seeming to be thinking on his feet as he talked. Sometimes, shifting from lecture mode, he would begin a dialogue with a single student in which the student was put on the hot seat with respect to his or her ideas, as Raths dug, with questions, into the student's mind, requiring clarification. What he said and how he interacted with students was electrifying. More important, he took me away from my narrow concern with reading disabilities and into a wider view of students presenting behavioral problems that were connected to "unmet emotional needs, lack of clear values, and diminished thinking capability." A whole new world of looking at students and learning was being opened, and I sat mesmerized, trying to hang on to every little piece of information being offered.

Rooted in his own scholarly research and that of some of his doctoral students at New York University and the Ohio State University, Raths presented us with a framework of looking at students' behavior that opened new doors to my thinking. He described three profoundly significant educational theories and their applications to classroom practice. Raths's needs theory postulated that certain acute and persistent behavioral patterns in children might be linked to unmet emotional needs. If a teacher first ruled out the possibility of physical factors as causes, it might be hypothesized that extreme patterns of aggressiveness, submission, regressive behavior, psycho-somatic symptoms of illness, and withdrawal might be signaling a student's unmet emotional needs. If, for example, a student persisted in extreme aggressive behavior, and there was no physical condition that might explain it, a teacher might well look to manifestations of deep emotional insecurity stemming from an insufficiently nurturing environment. When a teacher had made such a hypothesis for a student, and the data gathered supported such a hypothesis, certain teaching strategies could be used to help meet the child's needs. Under such conditions, research data suggested that the counterproductive behavioral symptoms would diminish over time (Raths, 1998).

The theory made sense to me. It provided me with a new framework for examining "problem" behaviors of children that would not respond to disciplinary measures and explained why classic disciplinary procedures were not effective. Raths's style of presenting information was compelling; he was a gifted lecturer, and it was not difficult for him to hold 80 students captivated in a small, hot, humid room. It was clear why students had come from all over the eastern seaboard to take this summer course.

Raths presented two more educational theories that followed his work on needs theory. Values theory used the same framework—the association of certain behavioral indicators with "unclear values." Raths's position was that the times in which we currently lived were filled with uncertainty, rapid change, and inconsistency and that in such a climate, it was increasingly difficult for children to develop clear values. Traditional value avenues were no longer viable: divorce was on the rise, church attendance was down, and leaders were more and more revealed as deeply flawed heroes. The stresses of living in an uncertain, rapidly changing society resulted in certain behavioral patterns, symptomatic of values confusion. These behaviors included apathy, flightiness, inconsistency, over-conformity, nagging dissension, role-playing, and uncertainty. When such behavior was seen in the extreme, and when physical factors could be ruled out as causes, a hypothesis of "lack of clear values" could be posited, leading to classroom interventions that provided a diet of "value clarification." Effectively carried out, value clarification would eventually result in a child's increased clarity of values and consequently a diminishing of the extreme patterns of behavior. Several doctoral studies were under way, and the data coming in were strongly supportive of the theory (Raths, Harmin, & Simon, 1978).

Of the three educational theories that were generated from Raths's own scholarly inquiries, values theory brought the most furor from the teaching and academic establishment, and value clarification was both ridiculed and condemned, with an intensity that elevated the debate to the level of rage. The notion that children were being asked to reflect on their own values and to make choices about what was important in their lives was anathema to those who saw "handing down *the* important values" of the culture to children as the right and the prerogative of adults. Accusations flew across the academy from New York to California, and attributions were made about Raths's motives and his own values. In a culture in which research would normally bear out or fail to support a theoretical position, academics took to polemic instead. The ugly value clarification debate waged on for years, fed in no small part by the work of some of Raths's doctoral students who parlayed their enthusiasm for values theory into personal crusades, reaping huge financial gains. When the dust settled, values education went the way of the Initial Teaching Alphabet, only to be resurrected in the 1990s with renewed vigor and again the call for values education (sometimes called "character education") in the schools. If in the 1960s Raths saw the climate of rapid change as contributing to values breakdowns, what would he have said about life in the first years of the 21st century?

The third theory for which Raths was known, thinking theory, followed the same framework—examining the relationship between certain symptomatic behavioral patterns and the "inability to think clearly" (Raths, Wassermann, Jonas, & Rothstein, 1986). Unlike values, "thinking" had no emotional baggage. Everyone was *for* thinking! The problem was that few teachers believed that lack of emphasis on thinking was a problem in the schools. After all, wasn't critical thinking a by-product of learning to read or do numbers or study science?

Impulsive behavior, overdependence on the teacher, inability to concentrate, missing the meaning, extreme dogmatism, rigidity and inflexibility in reasoning, extreme lack of confidence in one's own thinking, and reluctance to think for oneself were patterns considered to be related to a student's lack of experience with thinking. Not only were the schools NOT providing opportunities for students to flex their critical facilities; the opposite could be said to be true: Schools, ironically, were places that suppressed thinking, favoring instead compliance, obedience, and agreement with the teacher's position (see, e.g., Featherstone, 1971; Silberman, 1970). The ensuing argument in the field about thinking was not about the morality of Raths's theory; it was in the cry from teachers that "we do this all the time"—so there was no reason to worry about lack of thinking in the schools. This denial and resistance made it difficult then, and difficult still, to inject emphasis on thinking within subject matter curriculum at any school level, including in college and university courses.

INTEGRATING RATHS'S THEORIES
INTO MY COGNITIVE FRAMEWORK

What made it possible for me to listen to these lectures and take significant meaning from them, with respect to classroom practice? How were Raths's lectures different from those I had heard throughout my undergraduate and graduate coursework, most of which were mind-numbing and useless? These questions I have pondered long and deeply; for me, answers lie in the work by Donald Snygg titled "Cognitive Field Theory of Learning," found in the remarkable collection of essays in *Learning and Mental Health in the Schools*, the 1966 yearbook of the Association of Supervision and Curriculum Development. In his essay, Snygg wrote:

> Generally speaking, a learner will accept into his [cognitive] field anything which fits what he already believes but there are two qualifications: (a) in order to be perceived or assimilated an object or event must be necessary to the field organization; (b) assimilation of an event involves what another person, looking at the event from the point of view of his own perceptual field, would call distortion. Any item's value and meaning are aspects of its function in the perceiver's particular field at that particular time. (p. 85)

The term *field*, Snygg elaborated, refers to an organized whole, which behaves in such a way as to maintain its organization. Hilda Taba (Taba & Levine, 1963), taking a step beyond Piaget's theoretical conceptualizations, wrote that an individual in any cognitive encounter with the environment of necessity organizes the objects and events into her or his existing cognitive structure and invests them with the meaning dictated by that system.

According to cognitive-field theory, what a learner is able to "fit" into her or his cognitive map depends to a significant extent on the existing structure of that map—namely, what pieces are already in place. Where there are cognitive pieces that can allow for the new information coming in—that is, if the new information can be fit into the already existing structure—the student is then able to find a place for that new information (assimilation). The assimilation of this new information creates a new cognitive map, with a new shape, and a consequently revised perceptual field. When new cognitive pieces in the form of new information do not fit with the already existing map, then the information has no place and is discarded as useless or irrelevant. "The words of a lecturer will only rarely be relevant to the private reality and personal problems of the students he addresses and are very easy to ignore" (Snygg, 1966, p. 85).

Wannabee teachers enrolled in preservice courses in education who sit and listen to lectures about theory and "must do's" for classroom practice have incomplete, or perhaps "immature," cognitive maps, that rarely include firsthand knowledge and understanding of children and how they learn and very little knowledge and understanding of the complex systems and dynamics of classroom operations. That is why lectures about the how and what fall into the interstices of their cognitive maps and are useless. Bringing only my own relatively primitive experiences to my education lectures as an undergraduate, it is clear to me that I had also brought a cognitive map in which sophisticated concepts about the what and how of teaching would fail to fit.

What made the difference in my response to Professor Raths's lectures was not only what he said and how he explained the material; it was that my own cognitive map had sufficiently developed, based on 5 years of classroom teaching experiences and a broader reading base. By the time I got into Raths's class, I had developed a cognitive map in which the pieces of information he was presenting fit quite comfortably. I was able to assimilate ideas about children's behavior, since I had seen and reckoned with aggressiveness, submissiveness, and withdrawn behavior; with children who "missed the meaning" and were monumentally impulsive; and with children who were flighty and unable to concentrate. Raths's theoretical frameworks was congruent with my developing frameworks of teaching and learning.

Beyond the brilliance of his conceptualizations, I watched Raths's interactions with students. His responses and questioning strategies were like nothing else I had ever seen. My introduction to this interactive teacher-student dialogue and its significance in enabling student and teacher to drill deep into ideas and mine their most profound meaning began in that sweltering summer class.

In venturing an idea, you had to know what you were talking about; you had to take responsibility for your thoughts. You had to give examples, be willing to reexamine your position. You had to think. Raths had an uncanny way of listening to what you said and playing that idea back to you, so that you could examine it from a fresh perspective, as though holding up your idea in a verbal mirror. "Is that what I said? No, that's not what I meant."

There was no hidden agenda; Raths was not seeking answers. He was not looking for a student's agreement with a particular point of view. He wanted students to think for themselves, to examine their own positions, to support their own ideas with data. Some would call that "practice in thinking."

FACILITATION AND AFFIRMATION:
BUILDING CAN-DO SPIRITS

Raths often shared with his students stories about his own professional development, and I took them all very seriously. I particularly remember a story about a young boy he was asked to tutor in reading when Raths was a student in college. He told the boy's mother that he really knew nothing about teaching reading, but the mother, insisting that a college student had to know something more than she did, pressed Raths to take the job.

The boy's course of study consisted of taking long walks in the woods, during which time Raths and his pupil talked about all manner of things. One can only imagine how the pupil opened up to this interested and respectful young tutor. At the end of one semester of "tutoring," the boy began to show significant improvement in his reading at school. Having struggled with students who were unable to improve in reading, I thought long and hard about what magic had been done in such a teaching-learning situation. The whole thing defeated me, and I began to speculate that it was, in fact, a fiction.

It is only in recent years that I have come to understand the power of "can-do" and "can't-do" spirits in children and the effect of these concepts of self on academic performance (Wassermann, 2000). It is likely that a combination of causative factors contribute to the problems of children with learning difficulties. These may be visual problems, hand-eye coordination problems, or hearing problems. They may be problems of dyslexia—some kind of "cross-wiring" that contributes to written-language dysfunction. There may be serious or minor brain damage. There may be deeply rooted psychological problems. There may be problems coming from inadequate experience with books, language, life. There may be problems coming from negative feelings about self as person and as learner. To add to the complexity, it is likely that several of these causative factors are operating in concert in preventing children from learning.

Trying to track down with specificity what the causative factors are is probably a futile quest for classroom teachers, with their limited resources. It is, however, enormously helpful to be able to determine at least some of the possible causations and in which domain they lie, since this provides direction for instruction (Harwell, 2002; Lerner, 1993; Mercer & Mercer, 2000). Today teachers have far more resources on hand (although these may still seem inadequate, given the many and more complex problems facing today's youth) than we had several decades ago. Using everything that is available that can be helpful, I continue to think of Raths's student and their walks in the woods and how important it is for all students, and most especially those with learning problems, to grow toward developing more can-do spirits. There is no doubt that I now consider this view of self, in the learner, the key to effective academic and personal functioning.

I have seen children crushed by a steady stream of adult responses that diminish them:

That's a stupid question, Mark!
Why is it taking you so long to finish that, Alice?
You still haven't gotten it right!

I have seen children lose confidence in themselves as persons and as learners. I know that children have few resources with which to dismiss as irrelevant such comments from significant adults. Under a barrage of steady and continuous negative criticism, children become disempowered. They begin to believe that they are less smart, less talented, less capable. And when such factors underlie poor academic performance, it is hard to help children climb out of that pit, to help them renew their confidence in self and go on to become productive learners.

If I had it to do all again—that is, be a remedial reading teacher —with what I know now, applied to then, how would I do it differently? Assuredly, I would press harder for help for students presenting serious emotional problems. I would continue to carry out diagnostic strategies, to determine areas of needed help, and to design instructional programs that address such problems. I would continue working with parents, keeping them informed and up-to-date and enlisting their help wherever possible. I would use more language-experience instruction, employing, for example, key vocabulary, and organic methods (see Chapter 8, this book; Ashton-Warner, 1963; Raines, 1995). I would read more to children and give them books, along with audiotapes of those stories. While I would continue to work with building phonic skills using games such as Go Fish, I would not emphasize this to the exclusion of language-experience instruction. I would look beyond specifically reading to study evidence of behavior that might be related to unmet emotional needs, values confusion, and limited thinking capability.

I would carefully, carefully, monitor my interactions with the students, ensuring that no diminishing utterance fell from my lips, no matter what lack of progress I saw. I would carefully, carefully encourage and show faith in every child's ability to make progress— without resorting to falsehoods, platitudes, and phony praise of poor work. And, of course, I would take them for walks in the woods, listen to their stories, and be as affirming and interested in who they are as I possibly could.

Creating a Rich, Engaging, and Interactive Learning Environment

Highly competent teachers have made their classrooms alive and vital places for learning. There is a lot of activity going on, and it is purposeful activity. There is evidence around the room of students' work, and you can see that pupils have been and are engaged in challenging activities. Fresh ideas are continually being brought into the classroom, and curriculum experiences are initiated that have meaning and relevance for students' lives. These teachers provide for individual choice, pacing, and cooperative learning. The classrooms are intense, stimulating, vital places, and it is exciting to be in them.

MY DAUGHTER telephones from Nelson, British Columbia, Canada, to ask my advice. She has been invited to give a workshop for lay counselors who work with hospitalized addicts and wants to "pick my brain" about how to proceed. She has held the "ed biz" at arm's length all these years, choosing instead a career in business. She has had a long-term involvement with Narcotics Anonymous that has catapulted her into a leadership role, and she is often called on to help in the training of other lay helpers.

"What's the big idea?" is my first question.

"I'm not sure I understand what you mean," comes a familiar answer.

"Well, what are the important ideas you are trying to examine in this session?"

"I think I know that," she tells me.

"I'm sure you do—but this is your chance to rethink, based on certain criteria. For example, does your big idea capture the most significant aspect of what you hope to accomplish? Is it viable? Are you able to get this examined satisfactorily in the amount of time provided?"

"I'll give it some thought," she replies, open to the questions. "I'll call you in a day or two, and let you know what I've come up with."

Several days later, she telephones again. "That was hard," she says.

"I know," I tell her. "It's probably the hardest part of planning a workshop. But once you have the big idea clearly established in your mind, the rest comes a bit more easily. Then, all you have to do is put some flesh on the bones."

"Yeah," she laughs. "Now all I have to do is: everything!"

We laugh together.

"What I want," she says with seriousness, "is for them to understand some important guidelines for counseling addicts. But I think it is more important for them to generate those guidelines themselves, rather than for me to provide them. In that way, I think they will be able to own them, and they will have more meaning."

She is, after all, a child after my own heart.

"So how do I go about doing that?" she asks.

"Have you considered using a case study? A case would establish the conditions around which helping an addict is brought to light. The case would, perhaps, include a well-meaning helper whose strategies were inappropriate. This would then become the departure point for the group to discuss what kind of strategies were being used, why they see these as inappropriate, and what they would suggest as more effective, leading to the group's generation of more appropriate guidelines."

She likes the idea, and she explores possibilities for writing the case. Perhaps using a small-group format might be more conducive to thoughtful discussion about the issues. As the plan takes shape in her mind, she is satisfied with her role as facilitator, rather than disseminator of information, and understands the important differences in the two approaches for her workshop. She has been to too many workshops where information is presented but unassimilated, and she considers "talking to" singularly inappropriate for this group.

"What happens, though, when I get to the point of their generating the guidelines? Suppose someone offers a guideline that is totally off the mark? How do I maintain the role of facilitator, while at the same time being a judge of what is wrong?"

She is asking the right questions, sees that the role of facilitator cannot sit side by side with the role of evaluator-teacher.

"It's in the way of your interactions." I give her some examples of how this might work. "Suppose someone says, 'I think that it's important that the helper *tell* the addict to just say no,' and official guidelines discount this strategy as not only futile, but also counterproductive. What you can do is use a variety of questions that open this suggestion up to further examination. For example, you might ask, 'What do you see as some potential consequences of this strategy for the ongoing helping relationship between helper and addict?' And, 'What examples can you give of this strategy being helpful in the past?' Or, perhaps, even stronger, 'What do you see as some potential dangers of this strategy?'"

She quickly discerns how the interactive dynamic can facilitate further examination and how she can use questioning-and-response strategies to extract key guidelines to helping. She is already thinking about writing the case, and the workshop plan is becoming clear.

In this act of helping her to plan her workshop, I see how my approach to teaching has taken a 180-degree turn from what it was when I began to teach. For a long time now I have held the view that teaching is *educating*—coming from the Latin word *educare*, which means to "draw forth, to bring out, to elicit." How best to do this, so that students are empowered in the process, has been what has occupied my mind and heart for the past 30-plus years. The turning point, I believe, was that sixth-grade class at Lee Road School in 1960, when I took a giant step into the unknown, and nothing could ever be the same.

BACK TO LEE ROAD SCHOOL

After spending a sabbatical year in doctoral studies at New York University (NYU), I requested a return to classroom teaching at Lee Road School. Janet Allen, who had filled my position as reading teacher, was happy to continue in that role. There was an opening for a sixth-grade teacher. Although this would be my first experience with an intermediate grade, the familiarity of being in my old school was comforting, and the prospect of returning to the classroom, mouth watering. I came now as a veteran teacher (hah!), with one year of doctoral studies behind me. The plan was that while teaching, I would also gather data for my doctoral dissertation on "teaching for thinking."

Working with Artie Kelly, the new principal, I was able to select a group of children for my class who, based on my interviews with previous teachers and a survey of school records, had been identified as exhibiting patterns of behavior associated with "lack of experience with thinking." The remainder of the sixth graders were picked at random from the rest of the class lists for sixth grade. There were to be three sixth grades, and because of heavy enrollment, each class had more than 30 students. In the last weeks of the summer, I went about collecting data about the children in the "thinking group" that verified their inclusion in the study, sought approval from parents and the school board to carry out the study, determined that the children's academic achievement levels were within the "normal" range, and eliminated physical problems as causative factors.

A year of rich coursework, particularly with Professors Louis Raths and Alice Keliher, gave me new ideas for classroom work. Ongoing dialogue with other doctoral students whetted my appetite for a full program of individualized reading, and at Lee Road School there were no constraints on such innovations. As principal, Kelly, with whom I had had a long association, was supportive, encouraging, helpful. It was the perfect climate in which to carry out my proposed research and to try some new ways of teaching.

The 33 children in the class represented a range of competencies, abilities, attitudes, and skills. The nine children in my designated research sample showed very early on the behavioral patterns that former teachers had described: extreme impulsiveness; missing the meaning; inability to concentrate; overdependence on the teacher; dogmatic, assertive behavior; inflexibility in seeing other points of view; extreme lack of confidence in their own thinking; and unwillingness to think for themselves. Some of these children showed multiple patterns. Of course, none of the sample children was identified to their classmates as being in the study. The class was told that I was doing a study for my graduate work at NYU and that the children would be doing a lot of work on "thinking skills." They all thought that was very cool and immediately felt special.

Even in those first days of the new school year, I already experienced a difference in my approach to the children. Perhaps it was because these were sixth graders—more mature, more easy to talk to, more sure of themselves. Perhaps it was the change in me—more confident, more self-assured, more knowledgeable, now a doctoral student, with a year of having been part of the NYU faculty (hah!). But it was clear that my way of being with the students was different: more relaxed, more informal, less stressed about things like keeping to a schedule, or following the curriculum guides. Most important, I seemed to be ready and willing to give up the strict controls that had been a hallmark of my successful teaching in the primary grades. Controls had to be relaxed in a reading program in which children were going to choose their own books and work at their own pace. And if I believed, truly and with all my heart, in individualized reading, then why not individualized math? Individualized spelling? Individualized social studies and science? Could an entire curriculum be developed that in its application was tailored to the learning needs of each individual learner? I threw down the gauntlet and stepped boldly into the field. Not knowing how to do any of this, I nonetheless made the assumption that I would, somehow, figure it out. Cheeky.

The primary obstacle to carrying out this work, I thought, might come from parents. The parents in the catchment area of the Lee Road School were a particularly vocal group. They were intensely interested in their children and in their children's academic achievement. They were active at school board meetings and unafraid to fight for what they considered to be important for the school. The parent group, in fact, like the group of children in the class, were a varied and mixed bunch: from the more open and child centered, to the more conservative and perhaps even reactionary. It seemed to me a good idea to start the year by talking to the parents. Perhaps letting them in on my plans, and what I considered to be the educational value of what I was proposing, would be helpful in avoiding later trouble.

Very nearly all the mothers of the children came to an after-school tea. Mrs. Jacobi and Mrs. See provided refreshments appearing to be delighted to be called on to do this. I spoke to the parents about what I considered to be the importance of emphasizing intelligent thinking within the subject areas of the curriculum and about the importance of promoting independent learners, rather than passive conformers. I set this in the context of the kinds of adults that we all hoped they were going to become and their later functioning in an adult society. I answered their many questions and tried, nondefensively, to address their concerns for high standards in academic achievement. Upon reflection, perhaps the most important message I gave them was that I was going to keep an "open door policy"— that is, they were invited to come at any time, and in fact, I would welcome their visits. What's more, I asked that they telephone me immediately if they had any questions about what was happening in class. Assuring them that what I was going to do was be open to their scrutiny seemed to alleviate much anxiety. What's more, who among them was going to stand up and say they were "against thinking"? As luck would have it, the parents of these children turned out to be the most supportive group of parents of my teaching life; and I have attributed it to the fact that they were satisfied with how their children were experiencing their own growth and shared their excitement about school activities.

FIRST STEPS IN RELINQUISHING CONTROL

In order to begin the process of children's decision making in small-group work, I asked them to make choices about forming groups and gave each group assignments about "room decoration." I was not prepared for the chaos that ensued. Arguments were loud and heated about the most mundane aspects of the task. I tried to stay out of the process, except to play the role of mediator when a group became totally dysfunctional. It took the better part of 4 weeks until anything actually happened that made the room look more present-able. If you ever saw the horse that was designed by a committee, that is approximately how the room finally appeared. But it was theirs. I didn't know then that effective group functioning is a learned skill. Why is it that I could so easily assume that children will learn complex process skills just because I asked them to?

I see now how very easy it would have been to put a halt to the chaos, step in, take back control, and make specific assignments for work to be carried out. Teacher once again assumes control over all classroom functions—it's so much more comfortable and comfort-ing. What gave me the courage and the stamina to let the group process play out in that unproductive way? It seems to me that there is a core of dogged determination in me; some might call it stub-bornness or perversity. I had set my mind on this course of action, and by golly, I was going to see it through! I'm grateful for that core, for in the presence of group dysfunction, it would have been very easy to give up, to tell myself with conviction that "children cannot effectively work in groups" and put an end to the confusion. To my chagrin, I could see that the kids would have been happier to be directed, told, brought into line. It's so much more comfortable to be told than to have to work things out for yourself, especially when that is what you have been used to doing throughout your school years. But independent functioning is not bought cheaply. You have to work for it and be prepared to give it the time it needs to develop.

I hear teachers these days tell me that their students are *unable* to stick with a task and therefore must be given activities that are more entertaining, like the images on MTV—rapid, colorful and strident—to get their attention. I am sad to realize that this is an abrogation of the teacher's function—a willingness to bring instruc-tion down to a lower level simply because it is too difficult to take the students from where they currently are to new and more intel-ligent levels of functioning. Of course, it is more difficult to take this route, easier to rationalize that it is the students' needs that must be catered to. It seems to me that at the very heart of teaching is the requirement to open students' horizons, to help them move from where they are to new and more mature levels of functioning. But then, that is easy for me to say, since my venue is now my home office and my vision is idealized.

CHARGING FORWARD

It was a piece of cake to initiate the individualized reading program. With a short orientation to classroom protocols—selection, self-pacing, skill groups, individual conferences—the children took to the program like Canadian geese finding their way back north. Even those children with more limited reading skills were motivated by being allowed to choose their own books, especially when the selection—library books brought into the classroom with the support of the school library teacher—was extensive and appealing. Through individual conferences with children, I was able to get a growing idea of their interests, skill levels, skill needs, and ability to understand the material and to provide individually tailored instruction to meet those needs. Everyone was happy! This was working! Whew!

It was not difficult to design an individualized spelling program that followed the spelling workbooks but allowed for self-pacing. Children could move as slowly or as quickly through the workbook program as was appropriate to their individual needs. While choice was sacrificed to the words provided in the workbook, the idea of progressing at one's own pace was not only appealing, but gave children a small sense of control over their own work. Students would turn in work completed to the teacher; conferences would be held as necessary and instructional groups initiated according to common need. I considered the spelling program to be a routine of practice; for me, the serious indications of good spelling lay in the demonstration of skill in written work.

With reading and spelling programs now under way, I tackled the concept of how to individualize the math program. It should be stated at the outset that mathematics is not, nor has it ever been, my strong suit in school. But it wasn't math, per se, that was the challenge. It was the question of how I should organize the program so that it, too, allowed for individual choice and pacing, while attending to raising the skill levels of all. No matter which way I conceptualized it, individualized math continued to resist my efforts. What's more, I kept changing the procedures from ineffective trials, which made the children crazy. They not only sensed my confusion; they became justifiably confused in response. Encouraged to tell me what they thought, there were constant reproaches: When are we going to learn some math?!

In desperation, I told them that I would need a few days to work out the plan for the individualized math program—needed some time to think it through before putting it into operation yet again. There had already been too many misses, too many failed tries, and it was making everyone tense. The children were generous up to a point and seemed willing to give me a few day's grace. "Just get it right, Mrs. Wassermann, otherwise, we'll never be ready for Grade 7." Working evenings at home and breaking my brains to figure out how this might be done, I eliminated all math instruction from the schedule. At first, the children were mildly amused. After a few days, they became anxious. "When are we going to have math again?" It was surprising to me to see how programmed children were in what was "necessary" for them in school. I would have thought they would be delighted to skip math; nothing could have been further from the truth.

One evening a week, I attended a doctoral seminar at the university, where graduate students could talk about their research studies and get some informed feedback from the instructor. I presented not my work with the "thinking sample" but rather my anguish over how my attempts at individualizing math were failing. I reproached my instructor: "You advise us to individualize instruction but provide us with no help in *how*. I think this is immoral!" Our teacher was sympathetic and nondefensive, responding, "We don't know how ourselves." At least he was honest; the bottom line was that I was on my own. I had already committed myself to choice, self-pacing, and individually tailored instruction on skills. My beliefs, coupled with my determination, made it impossible for me to back down from the challenge. Or was it just plain old-fashioned stubbornness?

I created a rudimentary but viable guided self-study program based on the concepts and skills in the math textbook and gave each student a copy. They were to select those concepts and skills that they perceived to be necessary for their continued progress in math. I would help them make those determinations if they needed consultation. They were then to begin work on the math exercises and give me the completed assignments. From my feedback they could determine whether they needed further work on exercises on those concepts/skills, or whether they felt successful and competent in the area and ready to move on to new concepts/skills. The children were satisfied; they were working in math, and they were gaining an increased ability in assessing their own competence. Children with similar math skill needs formed groups for instruction on new concepts. Trying to figure out how to teach the students about reciprocals, I finally began to understand this concept myself. We were learners together. It only took 29 more years for me to let go of some of my fear of math to understand how a math program might be carried out that emphasized mathematical understanding more than just acquisition of skills (Gamoran et al., 2003; Marshall, 2003). I reproach myself for the limited mathematical functioning that constrained my ability to see beyond skills acquisition to what might have been possible. Oh, well. If I had wheels, as my grandmother used to tell me . . .

For social studies and science, I shifted to problem-based learning and project work. In 6-week time blocks, we alternated between a focus on either a large science topic or one on social studies. The large-scale topics served as umbrellas for small-group investigations. Topics were chosen from the district curricula but also came from my perception of group learning needs. For example, a large-scale science project on the development of life on earth was undertaken with small investigative study groups, each concentrating on a more narrowly defined aspect of evolution and each group presenting the results of its investigations in a large mural. Six murals, strung out around the room, made a stunning display in the wall space right under the ceiling. Another large-scale science topic on the systems in the human body also carried out through small-group investigations, each focusing on a particular system, concluded with sharing of creative projects that were designed to demonstrate how a particular bodily system functioned. Detailed poster-board diagrams showed human respiration; a three-dimensional figure, constructed of wood, showed the circulatory system. Each group presenting its "model" ensured that what was learned was sufficiently understood and was explained to others. The inauspicious beginnings of small-group work, undertaken with room decoration, had become more sophisticated, more focused, more responsible, and more creative. Problem-based learning appeared to be a good venue with which the children could engage in social studies and science investigations, and their enthusiasm at the introduction of each new large-scale topic was evidence of their response to this way of organizing for instruction in these areas.

When beginning a new social studies or science topic, the children and I always created the plan together, developing an overall design, identifying the areas of specific study, and determining who wanted to work in what group. It's true that I could have done all this by teacher mandate in about a tenth of the time. The discussions seemed to go on forever; and when it came to selecting groups, children would change their minds as often as changing T-shirts on a hot day. Yet something important was happening as a consequence of children's engagement in so much decision making. And the changes in their behaviors were becoming obvious.

It is true that in the first 4 months of the year, the dependence of the children on the teacher to "tell me what to do" was wearying. This was especially true when controls over the elements of *time*, *standards*, and *operations* are more and more given over to children who throughout their school lives have been habituated to follow orders, be compliant, be passive, accept what is given. It takes time for children to shift their normal in-school modes of behavior, to learn to accept freedoms and the individual responsibility that comes with those freedoms, to learn to choose. Jules Henry's (1963) stunning indictment of schools explains it:

> Man is yet afraid that unchaining the young intellect will cause overthrow and chaos. . . . The function of education has never been to free the mind and the spirit of man, but to bind them. Were young people truly creative, the culture would fall apart, for originality by definition is different from what is given and what is given is culture itself. (p. 78)

So it was understandable that in the first few months questions such as "What shall I do here, Mrs. Wassermann?" and "What do I do now?" were evidence of repeated attempts by the children to get me to give them directions, to lead them, to rechain them to my control. Yet new habits were being formed. After a time, when Eddie S. and Eddie M. came to me for specific and detailed help, they looked at me, stopped, and said to each other, "She's never going to tell us anyway, so we might as well go back and figure it out for ourselves."

Initially, confusion frequently reigned in small-group work and required a lot of teacher mediation, especially for interpersonal problems. Given all that I was trying to do and given the slow progress toward autonomy, I will confess that there were times during those first 4 months that I thought it would never come together. Franklin Segall didn't help either; he reproached me for not getting his math paper back in time for him to go on to the next level, for my inability to understand the more advanced math he was now doing. "Thanks a LOT!" he would say when I was tardy in getting him answers to his difficult questions. "I guess I'm going to have to figure it out on my own!" And he would storm off. And, of course, he did work it out. But why did relinquishing controls have to be so darn hard?

In the morning every day, the children would spend at least 15 minutes writing their plans for the day. There were, of course, places in the schedule that were mandated: art, physical education, and music—activities that were provided by special teachers in these subject areas. There were exercises in "thinking" that introduced cognitive operations and provided practice in learning how these operations were applied to subject areas (Raths et al., 1986). Afternoons were given over to social studies and science investigations. These activities were patched into individual plans; however, all other times were self-selected, based on self-identified learning needs. Children had wide choice with respect to when to read (do math, spelling), how much to read (do math, spelling), and with whom to work on assignments and projects.

How well was it working? From the inside, it was hard for me to say, since I didn't know how long it normally took for children to achieve some kind of independence, to achieve feelings of being empowered to think for themselves and assess their own performance.

With no textbooks to guide my own steep learning curve and no guru to advise, inform, or enlighten me about the wisdom of what I had set out to do or the teaching strategies I had, through trial and error set in operation, I had to make up the answers to my own hard questions. Philip D'Amico, who still haunts my dreams, had chosen *not* to do math. It was very obviously omitted from his daily plan for more than a week. When I consulted with him, at first he said that he would eventually get to it. After 2 weeks, I grew more troubled and asked more directly about his scheduling some math for himself. Having learned that he had been invited to choose for himself, and having learned that he *could* choose for himself, he just decided to *not* choose math.

I asked him, "What will happen, Phil, when you finish Grade 6 and move up to Grade 7? What will happen if you don't get your math work done? I'm really worried about it." He dug his heels in. Math was out. And I was caught between a rock and a hard place. Do I shelve the beliefs I held so dearly and the protocols I had worked so hard to establish? Do I break down and simply say, "Phil, you have just GOT TO DO YOUR MATH!" Does choice goes out the window when kids make inappropriate (to me) choices?

I suffered greatly and allowed him his choice. He was clear; he knew it would mean a failing grade on his report card, and he was ready for that. He spent his time reading endless books about fish and life in the sea, and he made the most exquisite and detailed drawings of all varieties of tropical fish. He knew the name of every sea creature, from the tiniest to the largest. He was enamored with ocean life and despised math. Who knows where Philip D'Amico is today, whether he has become a naturalist, a pet-shop owner, or a marine biologist, and if he is able to balance his checkbook. I do know that he did manage to complete high school in 1968 along with the rest of those sixth graders. Maybe he learned reciprocals when he was required to help his own children with their math assignments.

February came, and with it a heavy snowfall that made the roads virtually impassable. The main highway was barely open, and I braved the drive from New York City out to Levittown—35 miles of clutching the steering wheel and wondering if I could keep my little car on the icy road. It was nearly 9:30 a.m. when I finally got to school. I raced down the hall, to see Janet Allen standing at the doorway to my classroom waiting for me, shaking her head from side to side. Oh, no, I thought, not a bad report about kids that went wild while I was being late.

"I can't believe your class," Janet said. "The class president began with the class meeting, and they told their news. Then they got out their plan books and did their daily plans. After that, they just got down to work. They really didn't need me standing here, but Mr. Kelly thought they shouldn't be left unsupervised."

Franklin didn't even look smug; he just looked his usual intense self when he said, "I hope you weren't worried about us, Mrs. Wassermann. We just went on with our work, waiting for you to come." It seemed like a small miracle.

Treating children respectfully—turning over decision-making options to them and respecting their decisions—was paying off. Their autonomy was growing, and it was observable. They sensed it too; they sensed that something important was happening to them—and what's more, school was fun. In addition, as the year progressed, they were becoming more able to assess their own instructional needs, point to areas of skills needed, and undertake the work needed for them to move ahead. For me, this was one of the major benefits of what we had been doing.

I watch the documentary film *Why Do These Children Love School?* (Fadiman, 1992) with the same ideas of problem-based learning, choice, and respect in operation throughout the entire school, and I thrill to see how natural it looks to me. Penninsula School has been up and running for more than 30 years—and the success of its program has been proved in the performance of its graduates in later high school years. I would have been so comforted to know that then.

SEARCH INTO SELF

With respect to shifts in my own behavior, I have thought often and long about what made it possible for me to hold on to my beliefs that such a child-centered program would work. What allowed me to persevere, in the face of having to overcome the initial obstacles—particularly the resistance in children's behavior, their initial inability to function independently and their strident demands for my control? What gave me the courage to keep giving more and more power to the children, allowing them to make more and more of the decisions of consequence? What freed me from the need to "prepare" them for Grade 7, with endless worksheets, homework, drill practice—like what they saw in the other two sixth-grade classes? I wish there were clear answers to these questions. As I search deep into myself, I wonder how much of the change was the result of my own stick-to-it behavior, which I've already described, earlier in this chapter, that doesn't allow me to retreat, my own determination, my own pigheadedness about my beliefs, my own need to make it work.

It was 25 years later that I wrote "Beliefs and Personal Power" (1986), in which I made some claims for the relationship between deeply held inner beliefs that serve as internal road maps, and direct day-to-day behavior. In writing that article, how I managed to make those critical shifts in my own behavior became clearer:

> We behave in ways that tend to confirm our beliefs about self. . . . [T]he beliefs-behavior connection plays a dominant role in our sense of personal power. Such a sense of power is communicated to others in our behavior and has an impact upon their perception of us. To a very large extent, we are perceived in terms of what we are communicating about ourselves. (p. 69)

> Some of us learn very early that we "can-do." We hold these positive beliefs about self and they allow us to stride through life with confidence and self-assurance. These "can-do" beliefs provide us with a sense of personal power— an ego-strength that inspires confidence in who we are and in what we do. Our beliefs are held with conviction; and we are consistent about them and we are clear. We have developed competence as professionals and we feel strength in that competence. Our personal power allows us to be open and non-dogmatic. We see ourselves as professionals of value. (p. 71)

Somehow, I had achieved belief in myself, congruence between those beliefs and my actions, growing feelings of personal competence, a strong sense of personal autonomy, and a new respect for the competence of the students—all of which allowed me to shed the chains of teacher control and give decision making over to the children.

STEFI COMES TO CALL

Stephanie Wolmer, née Assael, telephones me out of the blue on a warm summer's day. She and her husband are in Vancouver briefly, heading up to Alaska on one of those huge cruise ships that anchor in the harbor right outside my window. Thirty-plus years have been added to my life since I've seen her—when she was a student in my Grade 6 class at Lee Road School, in Levittown, New York.

We arrange to meet for lunch, and I have no trouble recognizing her, her face bearing traces of the very young Stefi I remembered, in the body of a woman now in her late 40s. Seeing her now is like hearing the wrong notes in a concerto—a melody that doesn't quite harmonize. She hauls out pictures of her two grown sons, both older than she was when she was in my class, both in college. We chat

Stefi comes to visit.

about old times, and she fills me in, positioning the "kids" of that long-ago class as adults, around the globe.

"What about Franklin Segall?" I ask. That enormously gifted boy who was the bane of my existence—always "on my case" about my shortcomings: I was not strict enough, didn't give enough home-work, didn't have math material ready for him so that he could pursue more advanced studies.

"He's a urologist, a research specialist. Lives with his family in Massachusetts."

Of course. Shouldn't wonder.

"And your cousin, Lenny?"

"He's in Chicago, practicing law. Has his own firm."

Ah, yes.

The list goes on. Children I knew and loved, now 40-something, many of them professionals, the connection tenuous between who they were then and who they are now. I search within myself to consider if what I taught them had made any difference to their lives. This is the question that no teacher dare ask aloud, the one that haunts us. Stephanie is bringing me up-to-date, but the pangs of the memories nuzzle the present, and I find myself wishing that I could spend one more day with them.

Stephanie and I are now colleagues. She is a teacher who works with children with special needs. She holds a master's degree in education, and her teaching gives her much satisfaction and pleasure. She has managed to raise a family and pursue a career, and I feel a maternal surge of pride, while wondering if I have earned a right to that feeling. But she is here, sitting across the table from me, one professional to another, our previous relationship melting away like the ice in my glass.

She is unabashedly genuine and open as we begin to resurrect some of our history.

"I can't believe it," she tells me. "All those things that became fashionable later on in education: teaching for thinking, open education, problem-based learning, individually tailored curriculum—we were doing all of that back in 1960 in our classroom. Where did all that come from?" She looks into my face with serious, professional inquiry.

I myself do not know the answer. But the question stirs the memory of a chain of events that led me to that pivotal year in teaching, when I created a new role for myself as a teacher—one that was as unfamiliar as new shoes, and as uncomfortable, a role that opened me up to a different way of being with students, that eventually led to who I was and what I did. It was my year of living dangerously, the year that I chose to give up control and give decision-making prerogatives to the students.

I have searched within myself over the years, looking for *the* key experience that led me to that turning point, the moment in which I was able to shed the swaddling cloth that bound me in the traditional teacher's role, standing center stage, dictating the who, what, when, and how of classroom life, and embrace an entirely different way of perceiving and behaving in the role of teacher. It's clear that such a change did not occur in a magic moment, but in a slow process, with pivotal building blocks along the way, creating a metamorphosis so subtle that the shifts from larva to caterpillar to butterfly were almost imperceptible—until, with wings in place, I took flight. In that year of personal transition, learning to fly was full of ups and downs, uncertainty, frustration, and sometimes utter despair. But once I had shed the chrysalis, I knew there was no going back.

ARE WE LEARNING ANYTHING?

At class meeting, one morning close to the end of the school year, Gary Barnett confronted me. "I'm really worried about whether we are going to be prepared for Grade 7. Look at Mr. Biot's class across the hall. Every day they sit there, doing their worksheets, and they have hours of homework. They're so quiet, while we're so noisy! They are working VERY hard, and we are just having LOTS of fun. Are we going to be ready for Grade 7?" It was a very good question, and I didn't know the answer. I told Gary what I did know: that this class was the greatest bunch of independent, critical thinkers whom I had ever taught and that their skills would last them for all their lives.

When the standardized achievement tests came along, the children's scores topped those of the other two classes. In the critical areas of reading, related language skills, math, and spelling, the scores were well above average. What explains that? Was it because the children had become so self-confident that they were able to tackle such tests and ace them? Was it because the information they had been gathering all year paid off? Was it because individualized skills programs, even murkily conceived and inexpertly developed, were an improvement over the method of teaching the same skill to a whole class? I like to think it was all of the above; but mostly, I like to think that when decision-making controls are given over to children, they are empowered, and when they feel empowered and respected, learning flourishes.

During the following year, while I was teaching at Hofstra College, I invited my "old" sixth graders to come to the college to have a discussion with my sophomore students who were learning to be teachers. One Hofstra student asked my former class, "How did you

"We can handle any challenge!"

manage to negotiate the Grade 7 curriculum with all the schedules, different teachers, and routine that was so absent from your work in Grade 6?"

Eddie M., one of the nine children in my doctoral study, whose initial "rigid, inflexible behavior" was so extreme, and who shied away from anything new, taking comfort and safety in doing the "same things again and again," was quick to answer her. "We are such independent, critical thinkers, we can handle any new situation."

I comforted myself to think that was true.

Using Evaluation to Promote Learning

Highly competent teachers use many evaluation procedures to obtain data for promoting student learning. They recognize that evaluation is highly subjective, and they are undogmatic and open minded about using the results. They recognize the difference between evaluation and grading. Students' increasing skill in self-evaluation is an important goal in the process.

IT WAS LATE SPRING, during my 2nd year of teaching at Abbey Lane School, when I was initiated into the world of standardized testing. The school board had decided, in its infinite wisdom and over strong teacher protest, to administer a districtwide standardized achievement test to all first-grade classes.

On the scheduled day of testing, the principal came to my room to deliver the sealed package of tests for my class. She placed the package in my hands as if she were offering me the envelopes for the winners of this year's Academy Awards. With the package came her repeated admonition about explicitly following the instructions in the *Manual of Directions*. No deviations were to be allowed. Time limits were to be faithfully obeyed: 10:00 a.m., pencils up; 10:30 a.m., pencils down. Big Brother was watching us.

At the designated hour, along with every other first-grade teacher in every school in the district, I broke the seal of the test package and distributed copies to each of the children, whose desks were now arranged in rows, as decreed by the instructions. Two sharpened pencils were in the pencil slot on each desk. Following the rules, I saw to it that the children were bathroomed and watered before the test was to begin. The preparations alone were exhausting and nerve wracking.

My 26 first graders were a heterogeneous group of delightful, energetic 6-year-olds, and, by the spring, I had got to know them quite well—their strengths, their struggles, their idiosyncracies, their quirks, their passions. Normally spirited, they were now extraordinarily quiet, the stress in the air palpable. They were doubtless reflecting my own anxieties, for at this stage of their lives, they hardly knew the difference between a standardized test and an artichoke. It was clear that I had communicated my own feeling that much was riding on the outcome of their performance. Even in those days long before all American schools rose to the cry "no child left behind," the onus of children's performance on such tests was surely a reflection of the teacher's skill.

The test began with a list of vocabulary words that the children were to define by blacking in the space for the correct choice from among four options. By this time in the school year, about three-fourths of my students had made their way through preprimers and primers and were now considered to be reading at the "first-grade level." Four children were still chugging along in primers and were likely to move into first readers by the end of the year. At the far end of the spectrum, Judy F. and Benny C. were struggling to make sense of a few basic words. For them, decoding was still one of the great mysteries of life. As instructed by the *Manual of Directions*, I walked the aisles, ensuring that the children were making their marks properly and seeing that they kept their eyes on their own papers—not that that was ever an issue.

Jimmy T., one of the better readers in the class, took his time, carefully studying the words in the first column of the test booklet. I could see him struggling with the unknown words, bravely sounding them out and finding the appropriate match. By the time he had got to the seventh word on the list, his anxiety level had peaked and his face had turned a deep rose. I touched his shoulder to comfort him, and in response, he laid his pencil down, lowered his head, and wept. I was torn between my human feelings and the detailed prohibitions about intervening to provide help. I felt like a killer teacher.

Judy F., for whom decoding words was an Everest yet to be conquered, sped through the test as if she had been given all the answers in advance. She blackened slots one after another, never bothering herself with the act of reading. In less than 3 minutes, she had filled in choices for the entire list of 25 words. For Judy, the test was more like a coloring exercise. For Jimmy, it was a trial by fire.

When the test papers were marked, Jimmy's paper showed that he had correctly defined all the first seven words on the list—that is, all those he had time to complete. Judy, filling in spaces without a clue about what the words were, managed to defy probability and got 13 correct. Even as a novice teacher, I was able to discern that something was definitely rotten about the use of such a test and about the educational significance of the results.

MARKING AND GRADING

While standardized tests were a once-in-a-while phenomenon, and while my experience with Judy and Jimmy highlighted for me the problems in determining, with any validity, the performance levels of my students, I had no such reason as yet to question my role in the daily business of marking and grading students' papers.

Every day after school, I would devise a series of worksheets and workbook exercises that would be distributed to children the following day. At the end of the day, I would collect these worksheets, take them home with me, study the children's answers, and make appropriate red or blue pencil marks right on the paper. At the first-grade level, this was easy. Slash and burn. Check (√) for a correct answer; ecks (X) for a wrong answer. Add up the checks and put the number of correct answers in the top right-hand corner of the sheet. If all were correct, then perhaps "GOOD" was added beside the number.

To my chagrin, I used this simplistic and educationally useless method of marking and grading students' papers throughout my first 4 years of primary-grade teaching. If a student's paper had a high number of incorrect responses, which were pointed out boldly in my red pencil, I was troubled about the student's learning, but I never once considered how the return of the paper might diminish that student, might set in motion a cycle of self-perceived-as-failure that might impede future learning. Moreover, I never wrote anything on a paper that would enable the student to see *how* he or she had erred and what needed to be done to revisit the error and do the activity correctly.

Of course, responses on these worksheets were either right or wrong—another source of chagrin to me now. When did I begin to understand that real problems have many answers and that thinking about problems required viewing them from many different perspectives? Blundering around in the vacuum of my resources for evaluation, I seemed stuck on methods and strategies that were used when I was a student in school. I never stopped to question, For what purpose?

LEARNING TO VALUE ERROR

Many years later, I found myself in the staff room of a school where I had been visiting, sitting across the table from a teacher who was marking her fifth graders' spelling tests. It was déjà vu all over again.

I watched her eyes scan the 20 words in the left-hand column, her pen trailing down the row, leaving large red Xs across each of the misspelled words. Without missing a beat, she shifted to the right-hand column and marked red Xs on more words. Then, she counted up the Xs in both columns. Twelve. With a sigh, she wrote a large "12/40" in the top right-hand corner of the paper, while already glancing at the pupil's name on the next paper that would undergo a similar vigorous assault. Sipping my coffee and trying not to be intrusive, I continued to watch her marking paper after paper, slashing through the incorrect words like karate chops. Bim, bam, bang! Counting up. Sighing. Recording the number of incorrect answers at the top of the page and headlining in bold, for all to see, the extent to which the child had erred.

Twenty years earlier, this was me.

The next paper yielded a tally of 18 incorrectly spelled words out of 40. The paper was a bloodbath of angry red slashes. Hesitantly, I asked her, "Do the children get these papers back?"

With an edge to her voice, she said, "Of course!"

I couldn't help thinking that this was like a scene from *Crime and Punishment*—the sinners were children who had erred, and the punishment was the teacher's reprobation. I heard the sound of reproachful voices in my mind's ear:

"These children are getting exactly what they deserve!"

"If you are stupid enough to get 18 spelling words wrong, you'd better learn to face the reality of your incompetence!"

I couldn't help wondering if the mark was more than just an indication of how many words were correct and how many were wrong. I wondered, for the first time, if marking has a punitive dimension. Did I do this too? Did my slash-and-burn marking indicate my frustration and anger with children who had failed to learn my lessons? After teaching a lesson or making assignments, did I feel betrayed when the students did not learn what I had taught them?

These were terrible realizations—marking as punishment. But even worse was the awareness that at one time I might have believed that such punitive evaluation practices were good for children and that they might benefit from the humiliation of failure. Ugh!

It was a long, slow process that took me from such practices, to open doors about what evaluation is for and how learning to value error is instrumental in all growing and learning. Studying, reading, and reflection-on-action taught me many things—albeit in a learning curve with the arc of a hockey stick. But I have come to the point where I can say with certainty that harshly critical and punitive evaluation practices are harmful to children, that children do not benefit from the humiliation of failure.

We do not learn *not* to err from being critically rebuked for our errors; such actions, in fact, embarrass us and make us feel small. They are more likely to result in increased anxiety, and thus increased tendency to err, for confidence has been eroded and feelings of power to learn diminished.

In the years after I started teaching—when I was *really* learning how to teach—I never encountered a child who learned to spell better from such evaluative practice. I have, rather, seen many adults who tell me that they are abominable spellers, and this perception of self shapes their lives. I have come to understand the critical differences between being realistic about one's limitations, which we do with maturity and wisdom, and being humiliated by failure.

When did we as teachers begin regarding the absence of error in a child's work as the sine qua non of excellence? When did classroom practice begin to put major emphasis on numbers of "rights and wrongs" at the very heart of what is important in learning? When did we get locked into the belief that the hallmark of a child's level of accomplishment is represented in a tallying up of right answers? I wonder what is actually underneath such philosophical underpinnings of educational practice and whether someone who holds these beliefs has lost all sense of what's important in children's learning and mental health.

Error, of course, is a natural condition of just about everything we do in our lives. We take a wrong turn off the highway and wind up going back over the bridge from which we came; we put two tablespoons of baking soda into the cake, instead of two teaspoons; we forget to feed the cat before leaving for work; we enter a withdrawal incorrectly in the checkbook; the mail carrier delivers the mail to the wrong apartment; we dial the wrong number on the telephone; we spell *concomitant* incorrectly in a manuscript we have submitted for publication; we bring the wrong documents to the accountant; we measure the length of the window inaccurately and buy the wrong size blinds. Such errors we make every day of our adult lives, and while they are at the very least irksome, and at worst need our urgent corrective attention, we do not measure our daily functioning by how many errors we have made or how many tasks we have got right.

Much more critical is our ability to discern the problem and apply corrective measures—without coming unglued in the process. That, to me, is an important criterion of maturity and wisdom, or as Lewis Thomas (1983) has written, "our human capacity for blundering and the human gift for bouncing back to try again" (pp. 81–82). To learn to accept our blundering, our fallibility, as part of our humanness; to learn to accept error as the mode of learning; to learn to use error to drive us forward to new understandings; to learn to keep our courage, our faith in ourselves, our ability to keep trying— these, to me, are the indicators that distinguish us as successful, can-do adults. And frankly, I cannot see this kind of growth occurring with evaluative practices that are rooted in punishment for error, for such practices give the very opposite results. With such practices, not only are children not empowered; they become afraid to try, afraid to take risks, for fear that they will be wrong.

Now that in my infinite wisdom, as a mature adult I have decided to begin the study of Italian, I shudder to think what I would feel, in my lame efforts to build a vocabulary and compose the most elementary sentences, if a teacher were assigned to watch my pathetic struggles, monitoring what I did, assessing what was right and what was wrong about every utterance, then at the end of each day's lesson, tallying my every error. Well, I tell you, without a doubt I'd chuck it, convinced that I was too stupid to make any gains at all. It's also occurred to me that if young children learning to talk had each word and sentence evaluated by a teacher, the learning of language might be delayed by years—and in some cases, children might just choose to be silent.

WHAT'S EVALUATION FOR?

My introduction to the idea of self-evaluation came from Carl Rogers's seminal text, *On Becoming a Person* (1961), to which I was introduced as a graduate student at New York University. Rogers's "client-centered therapy" was at the cutting edge of a new psychotherapeutic movement, a departure from traditional Freudian analysis. Freudian therapy was concerned with uncovering traumatic events from childhood that were retained in the "unconscious" and that were seen to contribute to dysfunctional adult behaviors. Rogers's approach, and that of others who followed this psychotherapeutic pathway, were focused more on "self-actualization"—the building of positive concepts of self.

The concepts of "self-esteem, openness to experience and psychological freedom" were heady for us teachers, who were becoming more and more aware of the impact of negative views of self on personal and school behavior. Thus began serious quests for "building children's self concepts" in teaching strategies that would enable students to succeed and become more "fully functioning adults" (Purkey, 1970). It was a serious and noble aim, but like many good ideas in education, it soon became manipulated, torqued, and finally packaged, which reduced the goal to the level of games and strategies that were applied like cold compresses to a swollen ankle, without any regard for the deeper appreciation of the wound.

Rogers's (1961) view about the internal locus of evaluation resonated deeply for me, as I was at that time in my own struggle to step out of the boundaries that had constrained me and toward what I considered to be my self-actualization journey. In his formulation of a "theory of creativity," he wrote:

> Perhaps the most fundamental condition of creativity is that the source or locus of evaluative judgment is internal. The value of his product is, for the creative person, established not by the praise or criticism of others, but by himself. . . . This does not mean that he is oblivious to, or unwilling to be aware of the judgments of others. It is simply that the basis of evaluation lies within himself, in his own organismic reaction to and appraisal of his product . . . no outside evaluation can change that fundamental fact. (p. 354)

There are moments in life when one has an experience of crossing a boundary with no return. The experience has changed you fundamentally and has put you into a new cognitive territory. For me, that sentence of Rogers's about the locus of evaluation was like a smack in the eye. It took me into new cognitive territory from which I began wrestling with meaning and application. If I believed this, what were the implications for my life, for the lives of my students? What did this mean for the evaluative practices I had been using and would choose to use in future? Having come light years from my Judy F. and Jimmy T. standardized testing experience, I began to reorder my thinking about evaluation—what it was for, how it helped or hurt children, and what classroom practices were congruent with my newly formed beliefs. It took 30 years before I arrived at the point at which I could articulate my position on evaluation (see Figure 7.1).

A teacher's beliefs about learning and about students are the keys in determining the evaluative strategies he or she will use. To make evaluation enabling, teachers must truly and deeply believe in the importance of self-evaluation as a goal of education.

PUTTING SELF-EVALUATION INTO PRACTICE

Report cards descended on us at Lee Road School with the weight of a block of granite. The chair of the school board, a used-car salesman, had taken it upon himself to redesign the district's report cards. Instead of just giving letter grades for each subject, teachers were

Figure 7.1 What's evaluation for?

1. Evaluation is a process that provides feedback to learners to enable subsequent growth. For evaluation to be enabling, it must be affirming, rather than punishing; respectful of the student; and protective of the student's dignity.

2. An important goal of the evaluative process is to shift the locus of evaluation from teachers to learners, so that learners become more informed self-evaluators. This liberates them to take the steps that allow for ongoing, lifelong learning outside the classroom. Shifting the locus of evaluation requires that
   * The judgment made is personal to the evaluator and not an authoritative truth.
   * The teacher provides students with self-evaluative tools so that they may learn to make their own diagnostic evaluations of their work.
   * The teacher accepts students' self-evaluations, without assuming the role of final judge of whether the self-evaluation is "correct."

3. Evaluation requires the ability to make performance criteria explicit, diagnose weaknesses and strengths according to those criteria, and highlight what the student must do to improve his or her subsequent learning. In making diagnostic assessments, it is helpful to
   * Make the performance criteria clear to the learner.
   * Suggest how the learner might take the next steps to improve his or her work on the task.
   * Be selective in pointing out what is more important, rather than overwhelming the learner by attempting to deal with every aspect of the performance that requires improvement.

4. The evaluative process includes giving parents informed feedback about their children's work in school. Feedback to parents, like feedback to students, is more helpful when it is
   * Respectful of the student.
   * Clear in how the work meets or fails to meet the performance criteria.

5. For every teacher, evaluating/judging is a higher-order thinking task. If it is hard to do, it is because it requires much thinking, much clarity about criteria and standards, much analysis, much mental processing, and much well-developed skill in making appropriate evaluative responses. Because evaluative judgments are in the eye of the beholder, the illusion that evaluation can be objective is only that—an illusion.

6. Evaluation and grading are two different (and often unrelated) procedures. The process of evaluation is diagnosis according to criteria and provision of feedback that informs subsequent learning. The procedure of grading is assigning a quantitative value to performance and ranking that performance in a hierarchical order.

Note: Reprinted from "What's Evaluation For?" by S. Wassermann, 1991, *Childhood Education, 68*, pp. 93–96. Reprinted by permission of the Association for Childhood Education International, 17904 Georgia Avenue, Suite 215, Olney, MD 20832. Copyright © 1991 by the Association.

now required to make two additional determinations: the level at which the student was perceived to be working (at grade, below grade, above grade) and the effort that the child was putting into his or her schoolwork. Each mark would now have at least two dimensions: a letter (for performance assessment), and a number, from 1 to 3, signifying high, medium, or low effort. But some marks might have a third dimension: an asterisk (*) next to the letter and number, indicating that the student was working on curriculum content above grade level, or a number sign, (#) indicating that the student was working on curriculum below grade level. Figuring out this system for each child in each subject was too much for teachers dealing with the subjectivity of giving grades in the first place. Of course, the school board chair did not foresee (in the law of unintended consequences) that his system made it possible for a child who was making good progress in moving from working slightly below grade level, to performing at grade level, to receive a grade of C-1, where that child had, in the previous reporting period, earned a grade of #A-1. How could teachers convince a child or his or her parents that a shift from #A-1 to C-1 was a sign of improvement? It was "We have met the enemy and he is us" time.

Having come through 7 months of giving decision-making control to the children in this sixth-grade class, I made a mock-up copy of the report card and asked the children to grade themselves, explaining the new system as best I could. They understood it quickly—more quickly than many teachers—and took to filling in the spaces with the wisdom and seriousness that only children can bring to such a job. Once again, they thrilled and impressed me with their thoughtfulness.

Philip D'Amico, the boy who had abandoned work in math, awarded himself a grade of D-3 in math, which broke my heart—but he was clear that that's what he had earned. Margaret Zadikov depressed many of her grades; her belief that too much self-praise was not a good thing. Harold Pinzler gave himself a grade of B-1 for social studies, which I queried, with clarifying questions, rubbing the grade against the performance criteria in group and project work.

"I can't do it, Mrs. Wassermann. I can't give myself a lower grade in social studies. I've got to bring home at least a B, or my father will kill me!"

It seemed to me to be a good enough reason for the grade to stand.

Without making a single change, I transferred the children's marks for themselves onto the official blue report cards, signed my name, and sent them home. I didn't believe that I could have done a better, more intelligent, more fair assessment myself.

Prizing and Caring About Each Individual

Highly competent teachers allow students to express, and are accepting of, their ideas, opinions, beliefs, and feelings. Not only are they sensitive to and considerate of feelings, but they communicate this sensitivity in ways the pupils understand. "I am with you" is what is being communicated. In their interactions, these teachers' facial expressions, tone of voice, and language give explicit evidence of warmth, praise, and encouragement. Their interactions reveal their close relationship with students, free of attempts to dominate them. In these classes, students usually come away feeling a little better about themselves as persons and as learners.

"SHE'S IN ASPEN, you know? Conducting workshops for groups of teachers and acting in an advisory capacity for their new independent school," Jeannette Veatch announced the news like a drumroll.

I couldn't believe it. "What brought her from New Zealand? How come she's relocated to the United States?"

We were talking about Sylvia Ashton-Warner—the woman who wrote the seminal book *Teacher* (1963) and whom we both greatly admired for her work with Maori children in which she taught them to read using a method she termed "key vocabulary."

Sylvia had come to Aspen by default. Her husband, Keith, had recently died; she felt lonely and vulnerable. The invitation seemed propitious—a new country, a new school, a new environment, far from the heartache at home. She could leave her tragedy behind and do something new. A group of parents were opening an alternative school, and they wanted her, for her name, for the cachet it would bring to their educational endeavors, and for the direction she had taken in establishing a model of "free" education. It was 1970. The counterculture was on the rise; bureaucracies, with their imposed constraints, were suspect; and *freedom* was the new watchword. In the counterculture movement, the kinds of authoritarian restrictions, the regimentation, and the dull curriculum that were found in many schools of that time were considered anathema to freeing children's spirits and allowing them the right to choose. A. S. Neil's Summerhill (1960), a school without imposed discipline or structure, was the goal toward which other alternative schools could aspire (see also Ayers, 2004).

The educational goals of the Aspen parents for their new school, and the vision of Sylvia Ashton-Warner's organic teaching, were as different as turnip greens from mashed potatoes. Perhaps the parents were looking for an Aspen version of Summerhill; Ashton-Warner's "organic day" had a teacher-organized structure that provided for choice within that structure.

Regrettably, the reality of such differences, the overt pressure of parents, and the limitations of Sylvia herself did not emerge until she had already taken up residence in a little gray house, with a white picket fence, a few blocks from the Physics Institute building, which housed the new school. But that is another story, better told in Sylvia's own book *Spearpoint* (1972) and in Lynley Hood's biography of the lady: *Sylvia!* (1988).

On the basis of Ashton-Warner's international reputation, the school applied for and received a grant from the U.S. Department of Education that endowed small groups of teacher educators from all over North America to come and learn about organic teaching. To my amazement, my application was accepted for the first intake.

ASPEN MORNINGS

It was late September when Jack and I got into our little two-seater sports car, packed with enough luggage to last us for a month, and drove southeast from the Pacific coast to the rugged beauty of the

Continental Divide. We knew Aspen—that enclave of culture and sophistication tucked into the mountainside 8,000 feet up in the Colorado Rockies—where the affluent have winter homes for the snow sports and summer tourists come for the music in the Big Tent. Once silver rich, now tourist rich, with an economy based on snow, Aspen is remote and precious, abundant with the right consumer goods and the accouterments of the new monied class.

First Morning

On that first quaking-yellow-aspen-leaved Monday morning, I approach the gray house with the white picket fence, unable to believe my luck. It is more than a dozen years since I have read Sylvia Ashton-Warner's *Spinster* (1959) and used it as a text for one of my teacher education course offerings. Now, a member of a quartet of teacher educators, participants in a 3-week workshop sponsored by the Education Professions Development Act (EPDA), I have come to learn at the source about those "first hand experiences with teaching approaches and methods that preserve and nurture the inborn

Sylvia Ashton-Warner at Simon Fraser University, 1972.

vitality and imagery of children," as the brochure put it. I think of it as a professional orgy—Sylvia Ashton-Warner AND Aspen in the yellow season.

I am the first of our group of four to arrive. I knock timidly at the door and withdraw my hand quickly as I become aware of the slow cadence of a Schubert impromptu coming from a piano inside. Sylvia opens the door and says apologetically, "I haven't had my Schubert this morning"—this small woman with the wrinkled face and sad eyes, dressed in a white smock, black trousers, and black socks. No shoes, of course.

Two tiny ground-floor rooms have been set up for young children: an easel, paper, and paints at the window; crayons and felt-tip pens near the door; a plastic-covered cardboard box containing sand, set carefully on a plastic runner; another plastic-covered box containing several tins of water; a piano; a guitar; blocks of assorted sizes, shapes, and colors; a large chalkboard and several lap-size chalkboards, which had been irregularly cut from a larger piece; assorted pieces of chalk. The three other members of the team follow me into the room, with their frosty October-morning hands and their one-syllable names: Pat, Bill, and Tom. Sylvia warms their hands as she greets them and makes us some tea. We sit on the floor, tentatively exploring one another— four professional educators trying to remember what it was like to be 5-year-olds and feeling more than a bit self-conscious.

On the large chalkboard, a sketch of a carefully thought out plan used in what is called Organic Teaching, honed through many years of teaching in the Maori Infant Rooms of New Zealand, is there for us to study: four movements through which children progress during their first years in school. "Movements, not grades, as you have in this country," Sylvia is careful to point out, "because learning is a fluid thing."

She likes to posture; but it doesn't matter to me. I am caught up in the drama of the occasion, as are my colleagues, and even on this first morning, we are loving it, and clearly enchanted.

"What am I then . . . " she muses, looking out the window. "Perhaps a director? A conductor? Certainly not a teacher. I have never been a teacher." She says that with a smile. I never understood, until many years later, her disdain for the harsh ways in which she had seen teachers behave with children in her homeland and her refusal to be associated with such acts of disrespect and the diminishment of human dignity. "I don't teach," she tells me months later. "I supply the conditions." I don't realize then that such advice, enigmatic at first, is to become a guidepost for my own teaching.

Bill, Tom, Pat, and I, having finished the first of what would be many cups of tea (Sylvia operates on Bell tea, strong and intensely flavored, which she has imported from New Zealand), are directed to a creative activity for the Output period. Her method of teaching us is to involve us directly in the organic day—not by lecture, but by immersing us in the process. Has she ever read John Dewey, or heard about "learning by experience"?

Observing my new friends, I see that Bill has chosen clay, Pat is painting, and Tom is building with blocks. I feel stuck. It has been too long since I've worked in a creative, artistic endeavor. And wherever did those fears of touching a crayon to a page come from? Sylvia places herself on a low chair near the window, surrounded by the tools she needs to begin taking our Key Vocabulary (KV) words: a black felt-tip pen, a box of pre-cut white paper strips, which are about 2" wide and 10" long.

Because I am so intimidated by the Output activities, I volunteer to go first. I am not secure enough to try my hand at arts or crafts. She asks me to sit on her left side, explaining to me the reasons behind this request: She is right handed; if I sit on her left, I can see the way the letters are being shaped. For the next moments, I am her sole preoccupation. The others, engaged in their own creative endeavors, retreat into the landscape. She focuses on me and listens with rapt attention, as if we are the only two people in the universe.

"What name did your mother call you?"

"Selma."

"Do you like that name?"

Hmmm. No one has ever asked me that before. "No," I confide in her.

"No?" She ponders, her brows edging down to the bridge of her nose.

How will she probe this?

"Why not, I wonder?" The question is as soft as falling snow— not a request to pry, but rather a musing. But it shifts the scene, and I fall into my adult self and reflect on it.

"Perhaps it's because my mother called me Selma mostly when she was angry."

"And when she wasn't angry? What did she call you then?"

I am at once as entranced by her questions as I am by her questioning technique. Even though she is asking personally probing questions, I have never felt so safe to answer them.

"I can't remember."

She doesn't press, but goes on.

"Who do you love the most?"

"Jack," I answer quickly. I find myself shifting back and forth, from child to adult, in seamless crossings of the years.

"No." She sends me back in time. "As a child. Mother? Your father?"

"Grandma," I answer. Again her brows reach downward.

In a few moments, she has uncovered some of my dark secrets, my sense of security never disturbed.

We continue to talk together, I on the floor at her left, she on the little chair with her black socks against my knees. Touching. Intimate. I, with the hard professional core, am beginning to soften.

When she asks, finally reaching toward my first word, what name I am called by Jack, I tell her, "Watermain." She throws back her head and laughs—loudly, richly—as if we had just shared a wonderful, private joke.

"Watermain," she repeats again and again, laughing. "Watermain," she echoes as she goes off to find the glue. My first word is too long to fit on the pre-cut white card. She has to tack on an extra length of card. She writes in large, manuscript print and speaks each letter. I repeat after her. "Capital W." I trace each letter with my forefinger. She helps to see that I trace accurately. She gives me clues to help me identify the letters. When the printing, the naming, and the tracing are done, she holds up my word.

"What's this word?" She asks the pivotal question that begins the process of reading for the 5-year-old.

"Watermain," I say. *C'est moi.*

The word is then placed on the floor, the first of many key words to come from our group. I am supposed to be able to pick it out from the pile tomorrow. It is the beginning of my collection of reading words, and I begin to understand about stepping across the threshold to literacy.

I understand, too, that through the process of taking my KV, Sylvia has learned a great deal about one of her new "infants."

Bill is next to sit with her, and I try my luck at making a flower with some felt-tip pens. The effort feels forced, unnatural, to me. But from the corner of my eye, I watch the Teacher in the little chair near the window as each of us takes turns to give her our KV words. The pile of key words grows in the center of the floor as the Teacher grows in her knowledge of our inner selves.

By noon, there are several paintings, a clay dinosaur, and a complicated block structure. Sylvia produces a camera and asks Bill to take a picture of his structure, so that it, like the paintings, might be preserved.

Before we leave for lunch, we are held responsible for putting the Infant Room in order. We do this cheerfully. It has been a good morning.

Second Morning

By the morning of the 2nd day, the four strangers have already formed a group. It is another one of those special yellow-aspen mornings, the sun reaching down the mountains that surround Aspen on three sides. Immediately as we enter the little gray house, we are each greeted with a warm embrace. We feel welcome and important, more so when we see the products of yesterday's Output period on prominent display on the walls of the Infant Room. We have our morning tea and talk together about yesterday and today.

On our first morning, we experienced the first movement, or Reception period, during which the child is helped to "clear out his desires and fears." Questions such as, What interests you most? Whom do you hate? What do you want the most? What are you afraid of? Whom do you love? What does your mommy call you? are all "heavy" sounding to us, yet in the hands of this gentle, expert, inviting teacher, are never intimidating. Could I do that? What skill in forming the questions, and tone of voice, are required? What conditions will need to be created to ensure that a child feels safe enough to respond? There is a large difference between the warmth and safety of this teacher's manner of questioning and that of the teacher who is insistent, prying, and professionally distant from her students. To know what questions to ask, how to ask them, and when the time is appropriate for them to be asked surely is the very heart and essence of taking KV. I consider that in the hands of a less sensitive teacher, this could be murder.

In Sylvia's hands, the responses we give her become our KV—those words coming from the inside of us—our own "native imagery" brought to life. The words, written in large manuscript print on pre-cut cards, are found in a heap on the floor the 2nd morning.

One of our first tasks is to pick out our own words from the pile. We do this and see that this is how 5-year-olds begin to read. We read our words to one another and learn that this is a way to practice this newly acquired skill. For children, the words remaining on the floor are those that are not remembered, and they are discarded. "They are not the true key words," Sylvia explains. I am struck by the simplicity of it—the onus of failure is removed from the child, the unremembered word discarded. What "real" teacher would dare to commit such a bold act?

During the Output period of the 2nd morning, we read our words to one another, we paint, we work with clay; and a continuous stream of conversation runs through the Infant Room.

Again, one by one, we are called to work with the Teacher. She is careful to let us know that she is prepared to wait for us to come to her, if we are in the middle of something important. The respect she shows for us, and for our individual learning patterns, is profound. Her actions communicate that our feelings are prized by her and that we are more important than time or schedule. I am overcome with the thrill of what I am seeing and with the implications for this approach with young children.

During this 2nd morning, we are led into the second movement, a highly telescoped version of what would actually occur in a real Infant Room. The pre-cut cards are yellow, instead of white. They are longer and narrower, since they are required to hold two words instead of one, and the printing is smaller. These are the words that come from "outside" the child—from the environment in which he or she lives. Sylvia explains that the child is ready for the second movement when he or she is "cleared out." She tells us that the teacher will know this by what the child talks about in the conference.

Questions such as, "What did you do yesterday?" "Did you like it?" and "Tell me about what happened" invite the child to speak about his or her experiences. When *bratty Douggie* emerges, rather than *ghosts, skeleton,* or *Mummy,* the child has made the transition.

"You can tell," Sylvia tells us. We believe, with the confidence of groupies, that she is right.

The words that come from our group on the 2nd morning are *oatmeal cookies, happy days*, and *snow mountains*. They will be found on the floor tomorrow, as we search for and read them.

Later in the morning, we move into the Intake period. We copy our words on the small lap chalkboards. (Sylvia has a lot to say about the way paper is wasted in North American schools. Chalkboards conserve paper. These lap-size pieces are cut up from discarded large chalkboards found in school basement storage rooms. I wonder why more teachers haven't picked up on this idea.) We practice writing and receive some instruction in forming the letters.

On the floor are small homemade books that tell stories made from our KV words and from the words we provided in the second movement. We read these books to ourselves and to one another. They are personal stories, made from our words, written by our teacher. Her advice is to "release the native imagery and use it for working material." Making children's books takes too much time? "Get the parents to help," she suggests, "and any other available adult."

I suck in her actions and her words, as if she were handing down the Ten Commandments. To say that Sylvia was a charismatic teacher is an understatement. We were putty in her hands—all of us on an incredible journey into this teacher's way of being with children.

It didn't matter that, in its conception and design, vital pieces were missing from the rudiments of organic teaching. It didn't matter that Sylvia's theoretical conception made sense in a cottage in Aspen, but needed retooling and attention to the practicalities of classroom life to make it work in an early childhood classroom. It didn't matter that she prohibited us from taking notes—a prohibition that I defied, writing everything down that I could remember after I left the gray house each day. It didn't matter that her behavior was at times quirky and inconsistent. My professional educator colleagues and I ate it up. Teaching by enchantment?

Third Morning

The compression of Organic Teaching into a short, active series of workshops lead us quickly into the third and fourth movements. Teacher-made blank booklets with soft, colored-paper covers, containing blank pages stapled together, are our first books. The booklets are hierarchical in their makeup, relating to the stages of our progress along the literacy pathway. The first one has fewer and unlined pages. The second has more, and lined pages. The third has yet more pages, and these are also lined.

Our own thoughts and ideas, told to the Teacher in the conference and written by her on a card, are copied into our first booklets. These phrases and short sentences reflect our Aspen and workshop experiences. By the time we reach the third-stage booklet, we are writing our own short stories. When we need to know how to spell a new word, we ask the Teacher. She writes the new word into the back of our booklet. Thus, each of us acquires his or her own personal dictionary.

Arriving at the fourth movement, we reach the level of a new booklet. This one also has a soft, colored cover, but it is larger and has many more blank, lined pages. Into this booklet we write new stories, becoming more sophisticated and more complex in our use of language. The march along the pathways of these four movements is tangible evidence of our progress along the literacy road.

The days slip by, and the weather in Aspen turns chilly. The first snow leaves a thin dusty cover on the lawns, and the mountains that surround us look bolder in their new white mantles. Leaving behind the workshop format, we shift gears into discussion; there are so many questions remaining unanswered about classroom applications. I learn more about the activities of the Intake period and become familiar with the record-keeping system, which reveals at a glance the child's progress through the four movements. I examine the list of possibilities for Output activities: Writing, Teaching, Painting, Clay, Water, Sand, Singing, Poems, Taking Class, Walking, Other Media, Dancing, Making Reading Books, Teaching a Song, Blocks, Observations, Dreaming, Quarreling, Crying, Talking—and in my mind's eye, I begin to see Output time operating in our own early childhood classrooms—and I want to get home and see what can be done about initiating such a program in Vancouver schools.

TOUCHING THE INNER VOICE OF FEELING

"Touch the inner voice of feeling, and it will create its own style and vocabulary" was Sylvia's mantra. Clearly, she had touched my inner

"Touch the inner voice of feeling."

voice of feeling, and my Aspen experiences, although brief, changed me in marked ways. For the first time in years, I find myself sitting down to play the piano, during Output time in the workshop room. My fingers, hesitant on the keys, are clumsy in translating the written notes into sound, but I am unafraid to take the risk of trying. Is it the feeling of security in this Infant Room that has made it safe for me to try? To play wrong notes, without fear of being shamed? Whatever the reason, from those moments, the piano reenters my life, and I am glad of it.

After the first week, I begin to write about my Aspen experiences. I find myself writing with a different voice now, leaving behind the stiff, dull, academic prose that has corrupted my writing since my doctoral studies. Writing in this new style is much more pleasurable; I am able to experience the satisfaction of creating for the first time in a long time.

Bill Cole Cliett, one of the other members of our workshop team, reveals to me that he has also begun to write in a new voice. So this opening up has not been unique to me. But for me, it is the merest beginning.

ORGANIC TEACHING

My work with Sylvia in Aspen became the foundation for how I began to envision early childhood classrooms. Good-bye forever to children sitting silently in rows, filling in worksheets in primary colors. Good-bye forever to beginning the school day with reading, writing, and arithmetic. Good-bye forever to the basal readers, with their bland, colorless characters who never fight, cry, bruise a knee, or behave badly. Good-bye forever to those meaningless first vocabulary words: *Tom, Betty, ride, and, can*. These "tried and true" methods now seemed archaic to me—like something out of prehistory. I was convinced that organic teaching was a better way, so much closer to the developmental needs of young children. Would it meet the test of a field trial? To an academic, belief is not enough. I wanted to gather data to support those beliefs.

Of course, this was several years before the "whole language" movement was initiated, before it became fashionable to teach reading and writing based on children's experiences. I'm not sure that Sylvia got adequate credit for her pioneering work in this endeavor, but for me, her conceptualization of organic teaching and taking the KV were the forerunners of language experience (Carbo, 1997; Kamii, 1991; McIntyre, 1996).

I was very keen to initiate a program of organic teaching in primary classrooms in Vancouver. They were ripe for it; it was early days in the "open education" movement, and educators from all over who wished to research the "primary infant programs" of England were making the trek to the UK, where constructivist teaching and learning were being studied and then transported to North America. John Wormsbecker, the assistant superintendent of schools in Vancouver, welcomed me to his office, and by the time I left, he had opened the door to a 2-year field trial, involving a selected group of primary teachers. More than 30 teachers answered the call for volunteers, and from this group, based upon criteria that would allow for a wide sample across social classes, ethnic groups, and children's abilities, 9 teachers were chosen. There was no pre-selection of children for the project classes.

All the project teachers attended workshops taught by Sylvia (whose invitation to join the faculty at Simon Fraser University upon her departure from Aspen is yet another story; see, e.g., Ashton-

Warner, 1979). Yet it remained for each of them to figure out, based on the wisdom of their own early childhood teaching experiences, how to make meaning of the Organic Day, how to implement the program so that it maintained its integrity, and how to ensure that each child would, in fact, learn to read. From many, many visits to the classrooms of these remarkable teachers, I learned about what makes Organic Teaching work.

A Teacher Teaches

In my very first teaching year, I was lucky to be sent to Marjorie McCleod's first-grade class, to learn from her how to conduct myself in the act of teaching. She ruled her class with a velvet glove, but clearly, the children loved her. Her classroom was a model of harmony—the children were quiet, well behaved, and attentive to the assigned learning tasks. There was never any disorder, never any paper on the floor or spilled water, never any rancor or bickering. Just a few very quiet words from Marjorie would put an end to anything that threatened the social order. Watching Marjorie, I began to teach myself how to do the same.

Twenty years later, with a lot of history behind me, I got a chance to watch a master teacher carrying out her Organic Day program. Only now, I knew better what to look for, underneath the apparently seamless way her program was working. But more important, I had a better idea of what I valued in the education of young children. It was not about keeping them quiet and orderly. It was not about getting them to fill in the worksheets and complete their tasks on time. It was not about obedience and submission. A sea change had occurred in my thinking about teaching and about what education was for. Now, I could watch Maureen McAllister conduct a class, as if she were Zubin Mehta working with the New York Philharmonic. It was so subtle that it almost defied observation. But now I knew how to apprehend the subtleties and to appreciate the nuances of what it took to make such a program work.

Maureen's 6-year-olds were almost all Chinese speaking, with English a new language for them. Her school was a 100-year-old wooden building in the heart of Vancouver's inner city. Many children came from families who lived below the poverty level. You could never say that it was the "conditions" that contributed to the effectiveness of what she was accomplishing.

When I arrive, Maureen is taking Sheri's KV. I watch with admiration the way Maureen engages with this child, paying consummate attention to her and to what she is saying, as if there is no other child in that room. Astutely listening and apprehending, Maureen finally asks Sheri if her words for today are *flat tooth*,—a capsule of Sheri's fearful encounter with the dentist. Sheri is delighted and watches Maureen write her words on the card. Maureen takes Sheri's finger, and together, they trace the letters, Maureen pointing out the initial consonant sounds (f, t) and the consonant digraph (th). Critics who deride language experience for excluding phonics, who see the teaching of reading as an either/or (phonics OR language experience) have no understanding that good language teaching combines experience with word study skills, in a meaningful system that singularly attends to each child's learning needs.

When the sounds have been identified, and the letters traced, Maureen holds up the card to Sheri and asks, "What does it say?" She speaks kindly, with utmost respect—never as a command, but instead an invitation. Sheri grins. "Flat tooth!"

"Now you ask me," Maureen suggests. Sheri holds up her card and Maureen reads, "Flat tooth!" They laugh together and hug.

Sheri clambers from Maureen's embrace, eager to share her new word with her friend Judy.

Although I am entranced by the dialogue of teacher and child in the KV conference, I nonetheless remember to observe what is going on in the rest of the classroom. Without adult supervision, the other children are busily engaged in Output activities: painting, playing at the sand table, writing on lap chalkboards, playing dress-up, playing in the block corner, drawing, and sculpting with clay. The room has a quiet buzz, but there is no excessive noise. There doesn't seem to be any need to monitor the activities. The children seem perfectly capable of working on their own.

Of course, the children didn't arrive in this classroom with such behavior already in full bloom. Considerable work and teacher expertise occurs in preparing children to function independently, make their own decisions, make informed choices, and work harmoniously in groups. I despair when teachers tell me that "their students are not capable of doing independent work," as if this should come naturally, as if helping students achieve such a level of independence was not an important part of what a teacher needed to do.

It is time for clean up, and at Maureen's signal (several notes on the piano), the children, without instruction, put away blocks, wash paintbrushes, leave paintings to dry, and tidy up the room. I see Output working with a class of 24 youngsters. I see that it is right. The children go off to recess, and I note that they do not explode aggressively onto the playground, as do others from other classes. Is it their participation in Output that has made the difference? Is it true that, as Sylvia has told us, when the creative side of children is allowed to flourish, the destructive impulses diminish?

When Maureen's children return from recess, three activities occur. The more advanced children are reading story books. Some of the first graders work in pairs at their lap chalkboards, writing their words and reading words and phrases to each other. They will soon have their turn to work with the teacher. Another group of children is working with the teacher in a circle on the floor. They share their KV words, and emphasis is on the teaching of related language skills—phonics, spelling, writing, new vocabulary. After the circle group has received instruction, these children exchange places and procedures with the lap-chalkboard group. I listen to Maureen's interactions with individuals and groups. She is enormously respectful, caring, inviting, responsive, attentive, and never commanding—who wouldn't love to be a child in this classroom? I walk over to the group of children who are writing and I read over hunched-up shoulders:

An egg is to eat and hatch.

I am careful with a knife.

I have some cards. They are horrible horoscope cards.

I am scared of spiders.

A porcupine has prickles and it walks.

I like to smell flowers.

The Chinese are polite.

Fire pervention [*sic*] week. Don't leave old rages [*sic*] out they may catch on fire.

Maureen has put her own imprint on Organic Teaching, and her understanding of the what and the how make it possible for others to learn by studying with her. To me, she is Teacher.

Do the Children Learn?

When I wrote my proposal to the Vancouver School Board, the 2-year project had three major objectives:

1. To test the impact of the KV approach to beginning reading instruction on reading attitudes and language skill development in a group of 6-, 7-, and 8-year-olds from selected Vancouver elementary schools
2. To implement the Organic Day program as a way of promoting open education in primary classrooms
3. To provide laboratory classrooms that would serve as training centers for the preservice professional development of student teachers

What the data revealed was that children in the Organic classrooms learned to read as well as those in the control-group classes. Of course, that was what we had hoped for—that children, would, in fact, learn to read and would become skillful readers. But we wanted more, and we got it. The children in the Organic classrooms had significantly better attitudes about reading and writing, and they told us repeatedly that their work in these curriculum areas was pleasurable, enjoyable, and satisfying. Of the 24 students who spent their student-teaching days in these project classes, all but 4 went on to implement Organic Teaching programs in their own teaching positions (Wassermann, 1976).

HARDLY THE END OF THE STORY

The concept of beginning a teaching day with Output activities has permeated my own work, even in the university classroom, for I continue to believe in its power as a means of releasing creative energy and in freeing a student's creative spirit. I have observed, and grown in my belief, that creative work is much shortchanged in education these days, so preoccupied have we become with testing and measurement and about standardization—all anathema to creative power. In fact, I shudder to think that if I were to approach even an enlightened school board with a plan to field-test Organic Teaching today, I would be run out of town as a weirdo who was trying to destroy the competitive edge of our children.

Yet even today, it is still possible to find teachers who know about the theory and application of Organic Teaching and who operate programs that ensure that every child learns to read, that every child feels safe and productive at school, that every child leaves school at the end of the day feeling better about him- or herself as a person and as a learner. The ghost of Sylvia Ashton-Warner walks with us; and we are grateful for her legacy.

Unifying the Group— A Work in Progress

Highly competent teachers are successful at having developed harmonious working groups in their classrooms. The pupils care about one another, they have respect for one another, and the morale in the class is high. The teacher works to ensure that every child earns status and feels secure, prized, cared about, and respected.

I T SEEMED the right idea at the time—a sabbatical leave from my university to return to elementary school to teach for a year. The dean of my faculty was not amused.

"Why on earth would you want to do that?"

"I really feel I need to get my roots wet, John. I'm going to lose my effectiveness as a teacher educator if I don't get back to working with kids."

"But a whole year? Why don't you just go for a month?"

He didn't understand. Perhaps he didn't remember that it takes more than a month to establish relationships in a classroom, for teachers and students to "learn" each other, and to begin to move forward. I needed a whole year to touch base with kids and, from that experience, to enrich my teaching with my adult students. I did not want to become one of my own professors of education, who had walked away from the real world of the classroom, never looking back, and whose teaching reflected that absence of awareness of what real life with kids was like.

In the end, it was my choice to make. In August 1969, I put an "Out to Lunch" sign on the door of my office, packed up books, clothes, family, and cat, and drove down the Redwood Highway, heading for northern California.

In the late 1960s, Marin County was an aggregation of affluent communities that clung to the rolling hillsides of the coastal mountains just north of San Francisco. Populated largely by executives and professionals who commuted from the city, each township had its own special charms: tree-lined streets, quaint shops, California-dreamin' shopping malls. Add to this year-round mild temperatures, with shirtsleeve weather even in mid-January—you get the full picture of the California good life.

San Anselmo was a slice of geography strung out on both sides of Sir Frances Drake Boulevard. It was one of the few Marin County townships that had affordable housing for middle-class and working-class residents. And Isabel Cook School, on the main street, was one of the older elementary schools in the district. It was understood that my tenure there would be for a year. I came with a bagful of enthusiasms; after 7 years of college and university teaching, I could hardly wait to be with kids again.

Outside my rented house, about a half mile from the school, was a tree that gave us fresh figs until December. The small supermarket at the corner featured more shelves of wine than of canned goods. Neighborhood cars sported license plates such as **m benz** and **hot tub**. The smell of sage was thick in the air, mingling with the scents of eucalyptus and redwood. It was easy to believe that I was now in California.

WELCOME TO ISABEL COOK SCHOOL

A few days before the official beginning of the school year, teachers were already busy setting up their rooms and going to "orientation" meetings. We met the superintendent, who in an address to the entire group of San Anselmo teachers—about 300 of us—bragged about his district, telling us that the schools had libraries in which there were "many books." Oh.

Chuck Lavaroni, the principal of Isabel Cook, was an old friend and colleague; in fact, it was through his intervention that the arrangement for me to teach in San Anselmo had been made. He was quick to let me know that "no special consideration" was to be given to me, despite my university connection. I had no such expectation, but was chagrined, nevertheless, to learn that my assigned room was undersized and that he had packed my Grade 5/6 class with numbers of students with "special needs." This, he said was a compliment; he felt that because of my experience, I would be the best one to "handle" them. He also ripped my name from the teachers' mailboxes, since it had been posted as *Dr.* Selma Wassermann. He didn't want any symbolic differences to cause divisions within his staff.

The Classroom

The furniture in my room looked as though it had been there since the school opened—all hard edges, chipped wood, uniform. There was very little furniture or equipment that would make a room comfortable or minimally attractive. I set about pushing tables and chairs into groups, putting the teacher's desk in a back corner of the room. I removed the multiple copies of basal readers, classroom sets of English, and social studies textbooks and workbooks and placed them in deep storage in cupboards that were accessible only by standing on a chair. This made room on the lower shelves for the 300 trade books that I had signed out of the school library. I went to the greenhouse and paid out 2 days' salary to purchase some plants. From the storage room in the basement of the school, I retrieved an old piece of carpet, got it vacuumed, and used it to set up a reading corner, adding large pillows begged and borrowed from friends and relatives. I had brought with me some pictures from old calendars, and I posted these around the room, bringing some color into that beige atmosphere. Exhausted, I sat down to observe what I had done, only to find that the room still looked very much like an impoverished, unwanted relic from the past—definitely Salvation Army modern.

A line from the classic French film *Passion for Life,* spoken by a barber with obvious contempt for education, springs to mind: "Education is a cesspool down which public funds are flushed." If the tax rate in Marin County was the highest in the state, tax dollars were certainly not being lavished on public education.

The room and furnishings were only a minor offense. What was major was the lack of any three-dimensional equipment for children's use—no art supplies, no crafts materials, no hands-on manipulatives for math, no science equipment. Only hundreds of copies of textbooks and workbooks. It was easy to conclude what was expected to be the instructional focus for this class of Grade 5/6 students.

The Children

My dream of coming to California to teach children had not prepared me for what came in the door on the first day of school, and for what I was to observe as I struggled through that painful year. Even now, I can't explain the admixture—a large group of children with such repositories of inner anger that it took very little for them to strike out to inflict pain on others. I had not known the like of it anywhere, not in my own teaching, or in the observations of the classrooms of student teachers, or in the comments of colleagues. This was unique.

It is fairly common for "normal" heterogeneous classes to include a few children who "act out" and whose emotional needs are excessive. But in most cases, teachers can depend on a core of healthy children to absorb the needy ones, to serve as exemplars, as buffers, while working to help those in difficulty. I looked desperately for that healthy core; and each time I thought I had found it, it evaporated. Given a climate in which children were expected to make informed choices about the what, how, and when of classroom work, my new fifth and sixth graders simply came unglued—fighting with one other, lashing out at me, destroying materials and equipment. I didn't know where to begin.

To tell the truth, until now I have never, in the past 30 years, written a single word about this class. When the term was over, I simply wanted to close the door on it and never look back. Without doubt, it was the hardest professional year of my life. But hardships teach lessons, and in many cases, more lessons are learned from hardships and from things "not working right" than from smooth sailing. These fifth and sixth graders taught me much, and despite the wounds, I am grateful.

Barney sends me an e-mail message from Nevada. As a consumer advocate, he has his own business in which he helps to discover Internet fraud and educate the public about how to deal with these issues. The photo on the site only faintly resembles "my" 10-year-old Barney; this is a mature man, brilliant, organized, selfless in his caring for his aged parents, living a responsible and productive life, financially secure. If you had asked me to bet a nickel on such an outcome, I wouldn't have taken the bet. He was one of the children I worried most about, so deep did I perceive his unhappiness to be. There is nothing that could persuade me that I had anything to do with his current success. But somewhere along the line of his development, interventions occurred that took him from that troubled time to find a better way of being and doing. It wasn't that he didn't sit down to work at an academic task; rather, his work was perfunctory and gave no indication of his intellectual gifts. He spent most of his time in the early months of the year molding hardening clay into formless shapes, allowing it to dry, and then with a dull knife, chipping away at the form until it was dust. You could easily tell where Barney had moved his desk; there was always a telltale sea of gray dust on the floor around it. Eventually, as fall became winter, with imperceptibly different temperatures, Barney began to draw comics—showing for the first time the depth of his brilliance and wit. From these drawings, he achieved status from the group, but it was grudging.

Barney gives me news about some of the others in the group: Paul, now a firefighter; Steve, who works for George Lucas on the Skywalker Ranch; Phil, who was a basketball star in high school and is now into bodybuilding. I remember them with a mixture of curiosity and arm's-length affection, and I am satisfied to know that they have survived. I have no information about the others about whom I anguished:

- Ismael, whose parents sent him, from Iran, by himself, to live alone with his 20-year-old brother, a student at the University of California, the restrictions on his life as severe as if he were a prisoner (and in some ways he was)
- Arnie, who bragged about the devious ways he had of stealing "stuff" from the market and drug store and who was encouraged by his mother in these endeavors
- Marianna, who came late to class each morning, because she was required to care for her baby sister during nighttime wakings, since her mother would not allow her own sleep to

be disturbed, and who sat by herself, desk turned to the wall, jacket on, with the hood covering her head
- Bertha, frustrated, unable to contain her fury with me, unable to achieve the rewards she had been accustomed to in previous terms by knowing the "right answers" to all the worksheet exercises, unable to respond to questions that called for her own thinking
- Willie, who lived on the margins of poverty, whose hands and neck were never clean, who struggled to read at the second-grade level
- Roy, whose arrogance was a thinly veiled cover-up for serious feelings of inadequacy, whose mother had abandoned him to the care of his largely disinterested father
- Kenny, whom the other children mocked and called "retard" because his level of academic achievement was so far behind that of the others
- Howard, the only boy of color in the class—and in the school —who suffered grievously from the ugly racist remarks of and rejection by his classmates

The list goes on. But what was obvious then and now was that most of these children were products of acrimonious divorce and separations, some left to manage for themselves, dealing with shifting loyalties. Parents, brought in for conferences, told me stories that were hard to believe of child-rearing practices that were, at the very least, bizarre. The stories explained much, but did little to make my relationships with the children easier.

A uniquely troubled group of children, a time when counter-culture lifestyles were on the rise, adult mores and standards evaporating, adults behaving very much like teens. If my fifth and sixth graders were a difficult class, it was the merest tip of the iceberg of that strange time and place.

NEEDS, VALUES, AND THINKING

My earlier studies of Raths's needs theory (Raths, 1998) had convinced me that children's emotional needs played a major role in their ability to function in academically, socially, and, of course,

Children's needs play a big part in their academic learning.

emotionally satisfying ways. Studying the behavior of my fifth and sixth graders, and the information provided by parents in conferences, I was quickly persuaded that their "needs-related behaviors" were paramount in any teaching program I was to set out for them. Consistent, affirming, security-giving, respectful, loving interactions became the core of my teaching—my students sucked it up, but it seemed never enough. As though they were buckets with holes, whatever I could give them seemed to leak out the other end. Needs-related behaviors of extreme aggression and withdrawal continued unabated.

Undaunted, I initiated a program of "V-Groups" in which the children could come together and talk about their lives, their activities, their problems, and any issues that they were dealing with in the absence of meaningful parental guidance. Clarifying responses would be used to promote reflection and, hopefully, more considered and thoughtful choices. They were eager to come to tell, but the responses of children to one another (in spite of admonitions to be respectful listeners) made it difficult for meaningful disclosing to occur. Nonetheless, I pursued this and other group-unifying activities, as I perceived the need for students to achieve a sense of belonging in our group, respect, and caring for one another as primary to their overall health and learning.

The academic program I initiated was based largely on problem-based learning, on instruction based on individual learning needs, and on tasks that required higher order thinking. The principal suggested that I go to the school board offices to dig out any hands-on materials they might have stored there for math and science, and I brought these back to my room, filling up the little space that we had available. Movement within the room was an obstacle course; I could never escape the feeling that the 26 of us had been shoved together in a space designed for 15 brooms and mops.

Self-selected reading and personal writing was central to language experience; and spelling, grammar, and language structure were derived from these experiences. Science and social studies were centered in problem-based learning tasks, rooted in "themes" that I considered to be of significance to these learners. Mim Woodward, the fifth-grade teacher across the hall, was horrified to learn that I had rejected "Peru" as a field of study, in favor of "Streets of San Francisco." I did not take her criticism kindly; I told her that in spite of my choice, the building was still standing.

We arranged for many trips to San Francisco—to films, the aquarium, the zoo, the theater, the park. We did neighborhood walks and climbed Red Hill, where we could sit and sketch the view. We made our own kites and had a "kite-flying day" that turned out to be the biggest disaster in all of kite-flying history. We cooked; we went to the beach and gathered driftwood, which we used to make wood sculpture in class. It is Julie Kellog-Smith's piece that still sits on my desk at home—a fragment of one happy moment with those beleaguered children.

The needs of the children exhausted me, and I could not find respite from carrying out the task of assiduously working to meet them. Each day I came home from school, looking longingly to the bottle of gin on the sideboard. I could begin to appreciate how easy it would be to become an alcoholic, how the frustrations of teaching could drive one to drink. Yet the alternative was to keep the lid on the children, to put the chairs and tables in rows, to give them workbooks and texts, to keep a firm schedule, to restrain all talking and eliminate all group work. In other words, to keep them quiet, submissive, and physically immobilized. This I could not do. I persevered with my plan. In time, I saw withdrawn children turn aggressive, and I began to formulate my own "spin" on the needs theory. Was needs-related behavior hierarchical? Was withdrawn behavior more serious, inward, than aggression? Did a child have to "climb out" of withdrawal and become aggressive before his or her needs-related behaviors were substantially reduced? I didn't think I could live through it.

THE TEACHER IN THE PIT

Neil McAllister, wonderful colleague and good friend, used to tell me that living through difficult teaching days was like being "in a pit." That you had to go down there and climb up from it. Teaching my class at Isabel Cook School was like living in a pit. I was struggling hard to maintain my love of teaching, but I was losing it fast.

I had a true appreciation of what feeds a teacher—signs of success that what she is doing is paying off.

For the first time, I had a true appreciation of what feeds a teacher: signs of success that what he or she is doing is paying off. Those are the rewards teachers look for; for surely, rewards are not seen in paychecks or in the perks handed out by the school board. Teachers don't come into the profession for the salary or for the working conditions. They want to help children to grow and learn. And what if the growing and learning come in such small increments that they are not observable? How does one endure this?

How many times did I search within myself to consider if what I was doing was right? Was enough? How many times did I contemplate alternative plans? How many alternative plans did I try? But never, not for a moment, did I give up my belief in an approach that valued children's right to choose, to develop autonomy, thoughtfulness, caring for one another, and emotional health. I knew that what I was doing was right; but I had no idea it would take so long in coming to fruition; and that I would feel so defeated in the struggle.

I had hoped that I would be able to move mountains with my teaching skills, my knowledge, and my love of children and of the job. But I had to settle for considerably less than that.

We put together a Christmas play based on the then popular TV show *Laugh In*. All the children wore crepe paper Santa Claus costumes and made up typical *Laugh In* antics on the stage. Mario acted the role of the announcer and said that we were presenting a *Laugh In* Christmas show from the "Isabel Cool" School in beautiful downtown San Anselmo. Joe had a tiny tricycle, which he fell off repeatedly. We were supposed to sing a Christmas carol, but *Laugh In* antics seemed more in keeping with who we were. Putting this show together and making it up as we went along was the highlight of our year.

By late spring we had achieved something together. The class could now function in small working groups with little fighting, less name-calling, and more cooperative spirit. Human relationships had improved, and from time to time, voices could be heard expressing appreciation for a classmate's work. I grabbed at these gains as if my life depended on them. Children now lingered in the class after school hours, just "hanging out" with me and with one another— especially when their homes were not welcoming places. At one after-class session, fifth graders from the class across the hall came in to hang out as well.

"Who's the dumbest kid in your class?" one asked. (So it was not Room 5 alone that contained mean-spirited kids.)

Larry was working on his project and didn't look up. "I don't know," he answered.

None of the other kids responded.

I regarded that as a big win. In earlier days, they would have made much over this question, mocking their classmates and downgrading the less able. So maybe something was happening after all.

LEAVING

There was no way I could get around the restriction that bound me to return to the university in mid-May, 6 weeks before the end of the school year. I had to prepare the children, to tell them that I had to leave and why, and that Miss Docker, my student teacher from San Francisco State, would be their teacher for the rest of the year. I would write to them and hoped they would write to me.

They asked questions, of course; they wanted to know more about what my life was like back in Vancouver and if I would return to visit. If my leaving was hard news for them, I couldn't see a sign of it. They returned to their projects and group work and acted as if nothing had been said. Could it be this easy, I wondered?

My last day was a bit frenzied. Patti Docker had planned with the children that there would be a "surprise" going-away party for me. I was sent out of the room after lunch so that the children could decorate the room and spread out a feast of refreshments, which they had taken great pains to prepare by themselves. Cookies, cakes, punch; balloons hanging from the light fixtures. I came into the class, the children shouted, "Surprise!" and I pretended to be astonished. Before I could express my pleasure, they proceeded, as if one, to destroy everything in sight. Balloons were punctured. Cake and cookies were thrown around; punch was spilled. I stood at the door and watched, sick at heart; felt my treachery at deserting these children; and saw their feelings of loss in their response.

With wounds still raw, I climbed into my little car and headed back home to Vancouver, to my university teaching, where I could feel safe once again and where adult students would, at least on the surface, behave respectfully with one another, where I would feel appreciated again. But I knew that I would never again be glib about classroom life, would never paint romantic portraits of what it was like to work with children, never tell stories that suggested how easy it was to be a teacher. Those lies had gone downriver, replaced by the painful memories of my Isabel Cool days.

⑩

Building Habits
of Thinking

Highly competent teachers value the development of inquiry
in their classrooms. The curriculum tasks they use reflect the
deeper, more substantive issues and emphasize the big ideas
of the curriculum. The questions such teachers ask are concerned with higher cognitive skills rather than with the recall
of factual information. Teaching for thinking is central to what
they do.

ABOUT A DECADE after I finished my doctoral studies, in
which I investigated the relationship between "thinking-
related behaviors and the development of thinking skills,"
I went to visit my professor, Louis Raths, living then in Dunkirk,
New York. I had come from Toronto, where I had been invited to
give a keynote speech, "Promoting Thinking in the Classroom." Of
course, "Dudy" wanted chapter and verse about how the lecture had
gone. I told him that it was now more than 10 years since I had finished my dissertation and almost as long since I'd collaborated with
him on the first edition of the book *Teaching for Thinking* (Raths et al.,
1966) and that I'd given many talks to teacher groups on the topic.
And now, I was finally beginning to understand the theory and its
applications. I was not trying to be funny.

Complex theoretical principles are understood on many levels.
As each new experience is reflected upon, understanding deepens
and principles become just a bit clearer. The process is a bit like

exfoliation, surface meanings peeling away to reveal what's in the core. Through sustained practice and reflection on action, I was growing more able to go to the heart of "teaching for thinking" and to find meanings that lay beyond my original conceptualizations. Consonant with the advice of Richard Feynman (1985), I had to "play with it" for many years before I could mine its fuller potential.

PRACTICE MAKES PRACTICE

It seems to me that how we learn, although described in hundreds of books and thousands of journal articles, remains a mysterious land of unknowns. Of course, scholars and researchers have discovered much about human learning, but I believe there remains much that is still uncharted territory. Intellectual processes may be even more complex and elegant than DNA; we just haven't had enough research into the how of it to understand the many quirks and idiosyncratic differences between peoples—the conditions that allow some people to deepen insights while others bump and grind along, maintaining more shallow perceptions.

As I study my own learning processes, as I fumble to understand how I reach new insights and new awareness, Donald Schön's (1983) work has been pivotal in illuminating my thinking. He has helped me to understand what, for me, are key learning processes— reflection-in-action and reflection-on-action. These paradigms enable me to take what I *think* I know and apply it to make meaning from what I see myself doing, and what response it provokes. Of course, Schön only describes the process. He doesn't tell you how to go about doing this. That part you have to figure out for yourself.

To mine the gold of the thinking theory, it was not enough for me to continue to apply what I knew, repeating in practice established patterns. To go to the next steps to deepen understanding and to take meaning to new levels, I had to continue to play, to reflect in and on the play, raise new questions, and allow myself to see new patterns emerge (Hole & McEntee, 2003).

That is the best way I can describe the process now—although in retrospect, one inevitably invents one's own truths. And it would not be an overstatement to admit that insights grew more from fumbling around than from doing things well.

TEACHING FOR THINKING

Working with my sixth-grade students at the Lee Road School in Levittown, New York, I created a curriculum that "put an emphasis on thinking" by designing dozens and dozens of "thinking activities" to engage students' thought processes at higher levels of cognition. These thinking activities came from the operations of the thinking theory (Raths et al., 1986, pp. 5–24), and I had every confidence that in the presence of such experiences, the children would show marked improvement in their ability to think, which would result in more mature behaviors. In fact, the data I gathered in my doctoral research supported this. My confidence in simple behavioral measures to assess thinking-related behaviors and the changes in those behaviors over a 10-month school year now seem naive. My confidence in the power of thinking activities to do the job by themselves was also born of my innocence. What I didn't know then was that I was positioned at the merest beginning of my understanding of the power of the theory and its potential for building students' habits of thinking.

As I continued to work with the theory over the years with student and teacher groups, I came to two important realizations. First, students needed "time on task"; that is, they needed to be allowed to "play" with a thinking activity—to observe, discuss, hypothesize, examine assumptions. I also found that such play was more effective in cooperative learning groups than as a solo act. The second realization was that engaging students in discussion about their investigations, using certain teacher-student interactions to help them extract important meanings, had considerable power to further student thinking, to make it safe for students to think their own ideas, to take students to new levels of understanding, to open doors to later inquiry. It took the two parts—the activity and the follow-up dialogue—to complete the picture.

These realizations grew from my work with a group of teachers in Project Science-Thinking, a 2-year field research program, which my colleague George Ivany and I carried out in 1982–84, with a group of 20 elementary school teachers (Wassermann & Ivany, 1996). From watching these teachers work, I began to see how a teaching-for-thinking program could be structured around pupil inquiry and follow-up dialogue, to promote understanding of important science concepts. It was in Marti E.'s class that I had my first "ah-hah!"

Play-Debrief-Replay

Marti taught in an old school deep in the inner city of Vancouver. An experienced teacher, she had been assigned a bunch of more "difficult" kids, and it had taken her several months to see her hard work on building cooperative learning groups pay off. In her science program, Marti used hands-on, investigative play with a variety of science materials, thinking activities, and classroom dialogue emphasizing higher order questions.

On the day of my visit, in the spring of the school year, Marti announces that there will be science this afternoon. The children cheer, as if they are being promised a field trip to Disneyworld. Marti tells them about the work centers that will be available: Siphoning, Magnets, Floaters and Sinkers, Sound, Observing. Each center has much material for children's scientific investigations. The children are able to choose three different centers for this afternoon's activity.

In each center, I observe the children carrying on investigative play with the materials. One requirement is that they record their observations and any results they find. When the play time is up for their work in the first center, children are reminded to clean up, making the center ready for the arrival of the next group.

With fascination, I watch the children working in the Floaters and Sinkers center, where children are testing a variety of objects to see whether they will sink or float. I am struck by the absence of delineation between play and investigation, one merging with the other as "messing around" turns to experimentation, which turns to insight, which produces further messing around. It is not sequential or cyclical, but follows an order that exists outside "logic." I watch Jasmine "messing around" with a piece of play dough, flattening it out with her hands and placing it on the surface of the water. The dough sinks. No one tells her to do anything more, but somehow, she retrieves the dough and molds it into a little cuplike shape. It sinks again. By now, Harpreet is watching Jasmine's experiments, and he advises her to remold the cup, lengthening the sides. They are both working on the same implicit theory, and Jasmine remolds the cup and returns it to the water. The dough sinks, and both children are amused. Harpreet tells Jasmine to do it again, this time lengthening the sides so that the water does not flow into the cup. Jasmine concurs, and this time the cup floats. They are delighted. Sinkers have turned into floaters, and a theory has been tested. Harpreet and Jasmine pick up their paper and record their experiments and findings.

When the centers' activities have concluded for the afternoon, Marti calls the children to the carpet and engages them in discussion about their investigations. She asks for their observations and attends to their ideas respectfully. She listens and never judges, never calling an idea right or wrong. Instead, she reflects students' statements, uses clarifying questions and responses, and occasionally challenges them with a question that takes her students' thinking to new levels. I feel a growing sense of excitement about what I am seeing. The way Marti primes the children through her questioning strategies, to prepare them for further investigations the next day is, I think, brilliant. Now why didn't I think of that?

I have since seen that Play-Debrief-Replay is a model that not only works with Grade 3 children in science. It also has applications to all curriculum areas and all grade levels. Building on my experiences with Project Science-Thinking teachers, I continued to flesh out the instructional model, testing it in different contexts with different levels of students, learning more how to fine-tune the process. The more I use it now, the more I am convinced of its power in building students' habits of thinking.

How Do I Know It's Working?

By now, I have freed myself from the constraints of trying to find a way to assess, with accuracy, the complex patterns of behavior associated with thinking and use, instead, broader indicators—guidelines, rather than test scores. I suggest the heretical to teachers looking for ways to assess student growth in these days of standardized assessment gone wacky: Look to patterns of behavior. Use observational tools; keep records of students, of how they confront problem-solving tasks and group work and how they behave when they can't figure out what to do. Examine behavioral changes over time, in the presence of specific performance standards. Use these changes as indicators of learning. Students who are exposed to demands that they exercise thinking skills in their curriculum work and their interactive dialogue should become more cautious in framing ideas, less impulsive, more open to new perspectives and less rigid in their points of view, more tolerant of new ideas, more able to discern deeper meanings, and more able to deal with problems and situations that they have not encountered before.

I know that thinking tasks should require students to think about the curriculum content. That is what teaching is about. If, for example, a third-grade class is studying occupations within the local community, students could be asked to make comparisons of different occupations, observing and recording the activities of firefighters, retail clerks, construction workers, police officers, social workers, lawyers, and teachers; classifying occupations according to individually created categories; looking for assumptions in the observations and recording of information; and suggesting hypotheses about the challenges of different occupations. I know with certainty that this would be more productive in challenging thinking than merely reading information from a textbook about job descriptions.

I also know that after groups of students work cooperatively on a curriculum task requiring them to think, subsequent engagement in an interactive dialogue sustains and extends their thinking about the data, the issues, the assumptions, the processes; brings richer and deeper understanding of issues; and builds habits of thinking.

Yeh. That works.

THE NATURE OF QUESTIONS

I began to study the impact of questioning strategies when I learned about the work of Ted Parsons (1971), then at the University of California, Berkeley. Parsons never published his work—perhaps because it was too unwieldy to be practical—and today, he is largely unrecognized. But he was among the first to identify differences in types of questions, establishing a grid that allowed teachers' questions to be categorized according to the kind of thinking they elicited from students.

Of course, very few new ideas come from the ether. Most are built on the scholarly activities and thinking of those who have gone before us, and it is doubtless the case that Parsons was influenced by Ned Flanders (1970) and by the much heralded work of Benjamin Bloom (1956). Be that as it may, Parsons pointed me in the direction of looking at questions in categories: those that elicit information (lower order) and those that challenge thinking (higher order). As he continued to examine the nature of classroom discourse, his grids became much more complicated; finally, so much analysis was required in the observation of a single classroom discussion that the methodology became unworkable. If this was a way for teachers to study their own questioning strategies, then the heck with it. What teacher has that kind of time!

Working at first with Parsons's analysis grids, I began to think about how to categorize questions more simply. After many, many field trials, revisions, and modifications, I was able to generate a new method of analysis to help teachers examine their questioning strategies. The "Teaching for Thinking Analysis Worksheet" identifies the kinds of questions that promote or shut down a student's thinking processes. An adaptation of the worksheet is shown in Figure 10.1, for those who wish to look further at this simple system that took only half a lifetime to develop.

The analysis worksheet is only a small part of the picture. It was, however, the launching pad that took me into deeper examinations of teachers' questions and ongoing study of the interactive dialogue.

THE ART OF QUESTIONING

My continuing observations of teacher-student discourse taught me that questions may be grouped in ways other than the "higher order" and the "lower order" classifications. They also have potential to provoke powerful emotional responses, which are likely to affect, substantially, a student's subsequent verbal response. Once I had looked beyond the higher order and lower order classifications, I was able to discern other useful categories that contribute to or diminish the productivity of classroom discourse. From studying hundreds of classroom discussions, I could see that some questions are helpful, and some are hurtful. There are questions that carry an emotional burden. There are questions that are digressions from the main ideas. And there are levels of questions that produce greater and greater challenges to thinking. To understand the differences

Figure 10.1. Analysis of teacher responses in teacher–student interactions.

A. RESPONSES THAT INHIBIT THINKING

1. Responses that bring closure:
Agrees/disagrees with student's idea
Doesn't give student a chance to think
Tells student what s/he (teacher) thinks
Talks too much/explains it his/her way
Cuts student off
Other closure responses

2. Responses that promote fear:
Heckles/is sarcastic/puts down idea

B. RESPONSES THAT LIMIT STUDENT THINKING
Looks for single, correct answer
Leads student to "correct" answer
Tells student what to do
Gives information

C. RESPONSES THAT ENCOURAGE THINKING

1. Responses that encourage reexamination of the idea:
Saying the idea back to student
Paraphrasing
Interpreting
Asking for more information, e.g., "Tell me a little more about that," or "Help me to understand what you mean"

2. Responses that call for analysis of the idea:
Give me an example.
What assumptions are being made?
Why do you suppose that is good?
What alternatives have you considered?
How does (that) compare with (this)?
How might that data be classified?
What data support your idea?

3. Responses that challenge:
What hypotheses can you suggest?
How do you interpret that?
What criteria are you using?
How would those principles be applied in this situation?
What predictions can be made based on that data?
How would you test that theory?
What new scheme/plan can you envision for that situation?

4. Responses that accept a student's idea nonjudgmentally:
I see.
Thank you.

D. RESPONSES UNRELATED TO DEBRIEFING THE BIG IDEAS
Classroom/behavior-management responses
Speech mannerisms

Note: Adapted from Wassermann & Ivany, 1996, p. 111.

in questions posed, their potential power for productive discourse, and their potential effects on thinking and feeling and to apply all this knowledge in a discussion, is, for me, the art of questioning.

I have come to understand that questioning is more than making interrogative demands. If classroom discussions are to bear intellectual fruit, with students examining issues intelligently, my questions must be sensitive to many aspects of the interactive process. This includes an awareness of how questions are framed. Some are put together in a way that calls for students' examination of important issues. Some are framed in a way that provokes anxiety, thereby influencing the nature of a student's response. I need to be able to discern the difference, to reflect-in-action, as I listen to what is coming out of my mouth and appreciate how those words affect the student and his or her response. This I learn to study, as if it is a life-giving source.

I find that good questions follow an interactive rhythm that produces reflection and doesn't feel like an interrogation. (The Italian word for *question* is *la domanda*—and some questions do, in fact, feel as if they are making a demand.) I try to formulate questions that allow for students' continued examination of the issues, that are clear in what they are asking students to think about and not so broad or abstract that they defeat the process of thoughtful examination. I try to use questions that invite, not command, so that I can build trust in the interactive relationship.

As I continued to learn the art of questioning, I found that I needed to keep in mind the purpose of my question: Do I want to find out what students know? Or do I want them to use what they know to arrive at some better understanding? Questions that call for students to remember serve one purpose; questions that call for students to apply learned principles to new situations are a different breed. Learning about both, when to use which, and being clear about the intended results created yet another challenge in helping me learn the art of questioning.

Here is an example of these strategies in a discussion about the Zuni Indians:

ME: Tell me what observations you made about the ways of life of the Zuni.

TAMAR: Well, they were primarily agricultural.

Now, I have some options. If I ask a question at this point, for example, "What other observations have you made about them?" the question immediately shifts the discourse away from the further examination of the student's idea that the Zuni's way of life is agricultural, to other aspects of their way of life. I instead choose:

ME: Tell me more about how being agricultural marked their lives.

By responding directly to the student's statement, I call for Tamar to think about it more. I do this for several reasons: First, such a response communicates that I have heard her idea. Second, when I play the idea back to her, she must take ownership for what she has said. Students are required now to think before they speak; they are learning that what they say is going to be used for further working material.

I continue to struggle to weave all these threads of questioning strategies in an interactive dialogue, while at the same time, I am attending carefully to a student's response so that I may formulate the follow-up response. These skills have been consciously chosen and practiced over half a lifetime of professional development. For me, they hold considerable teaching power.

It was a surprise that students initially would not be grateful for such a learning experience. My questions had no clear-cut answers! They were being asked to think! Thinking was hard work! They felt uncomfortable, frustrated, challenged, angry. For students who live their school lives in the black-and-white world of certainty, high levels of anxiety are created by questions for which there are no single right answers and that elevate uncertainty and ambiguity. Students long for closure, as do many adults. To know, with certainty, is very comforting. To live in a world of ambiguity is very unsettling. To think means living with uncertainty. We are being asked to suspend judgment, weigh data, and keep open minds before reaching conclusions. Students who are not accustomed to this process may understandably balk at having to think their own ideas, use their own minds. As Bobby M. told me, frustrated out of his head in Grade 6: "It's YOUR job to tell us what to think. You're the teacher!"

OK. So the road to productive discussion teaching is not a smooth one. But the payoff is rich. My experience tells me that once students have crossed the bridge and become more thoughtful, once they have tasted the freedom of thinking for themselves, they are truly empowered and there is no going back. Ever.

Preparing for Discussion Teaching

Every time I go into a class discussion, I spend a few hours preparing in advance. I study the material that we are going to discuss, and if it is a written work, like a case, I underline important passages that seem to me to be critical to the issues. I reexamine the big ideas, making sure that they are clear in my head, sharply focused. I generate a brief list of questions that are derived from the big ideas—sequencing them so that they begin with data-gathering questions, moving to analysis questions, then to evaluative questions, and finally, to action questions (see Chapter 11 for further discussion on this aspect of questioning). These questions are my "crib sheet," and the students are forgiving if I have to refer to them during the discussion, especially when things get heated, which they often do. My list of questions helps me to regain my focus and keeps the discussion centered on the big ideas.

The following guidelines, adopted as my personal mantra, have helped me through hundreds of classroom discussions, on as many topics and cases:

1. Know the students. When I know the students, it helps me to determine what kinds of questions are most likely to be productive for them and which questions draw on students' particular experiences.
2. Listen to and be clear about what the student is saying. I work hard to comprehend what is being said; if I don't understand at first, I ask for clarification. It is important to me to get the student's idea accurately positioned in my mind. As I listen, I am already beginning to formulate a response that will be a clear reflection of the student's statement.
3. Use a response that calls for the examination of the idea from a fresh perspective.
4. Choose a follow-up response that takes the student's thinking one step further.
5. Decide when the interactive dialogue with that student is "finished," when it is time to move on to the next student. Too much

time with one student will be too "heavy," and perhaps cause the others to feel out of the loop; too little time doesn't give me a chance to work the ideas. How do I know when to move on? Yeh.

6. Frame questions and responses so that they are always respect-ful, nonthreatening, and productive.

7. Know which kinds of questions are more effective with which students. When my grandson Simon, still in knickers, was fix-ated on the mountains surrounding the lake, I asked him, "How do you suppose those mountains got there?" He balked at the question—too hard, too challenging, too risky. I saw how it had misfired. So I tried to rephrase, asking, "I wonder if you have any theories about it?" At the invitation to invent theories, he was able to hypothesize that it might be that small pebbles even-tually grew up into mountains. (I like to call it the small-pebble theory.) So slight a difference in the question, yet so important in enabling a response when a child is feeling vulnerable.

8. Know the right time to challenge a student's thinking. Too much, too soon, too hard—it backfires, and as one student told me, "makes me feel stupid." Timing, as they say, is everything. This I learned from the hard experience of trial and error.

9. Know when to shift gears into the territory of the next big idea. Here again, I find that timing is everything. Spending too much time on one issue will exhaust it, and there will be no time left for examining other issues. How do I know when? Hmmm. . . . I just keep trying and sometimes it works.

10. Refrain from making judgments. Avoid like the plague "Good idea" and even "That's interesting." Arriving at this took me about 100 years of practice, but I think I'm finally getting the hang of it.

11. Work the interactive dialogue so that meanings are searched for, understandings grow, students' thinking about the issues occurs, and students feel safe in offering their ideas.

12. Don't expect miracles at first. Productive class discussions take time to grow—both from the teachers' and from the students' perspectives. Allow the time needed for self and students to de-velop the skills necessary for effective functioning. Be generous and forgiving of self in the process of learning.

How long did it take me to get to this point in orchestrating a classroom discussion? Like learning to play the Bach Goldberg

Variations, one never stops learning. It was an ongoing process of listening to myself, studying what I had done, reflecting afterward on what I had said to see what I might have said instead, thinking about how I might have changed it.

When I've had a very good class discussion, I lie awake at night dissecting it. And when I've had a perfectly awful class discussion, I lie awake at night dissecting it.

RELINQUISHING CONTROL: IT'S NOT FOR EVERY TEACHER

There are a few attributes that I have inherited from my mother, some of which I've embraced wholeheartedly, among them a passion for good food and a love of the movies. Others that I absorbed from the day-to-day fallout of her behavior I had to work consciously to shed—her obsession with perfection in housecleaning, for one, and her need for control, for another. I am now comfortable with leaving a newspaper lying on the table, dust on the bookshelf, or a pair of shoes near the bed, without rushing over to "tidy" the place. A small amount of "disorder" in my home environment no longer threatens my sense of security.

I had to work harder to unload other expressions of my need for control—much harder. Without doing that, I would never have been able to stand on the sidelines, as an observer of children's (or adult learners') play, without rushing in to take charge when they were carrying out investigations that I thought unproductive. ("Here, Jenny, why don't you try it this way?") From where I sit now, I can look back over a long teaching career and identify the need for control that was at the root of my early teaching days and see how instrumental it was in the decisions I took about my educational practices. I never questioned its existence, operating on the unspoken assumption that children were meant to be controlled and that my job was to manage and control them. It never occurred to me that such need for control was largely mine, that I needed control to give me a sense of security, and that, in fact, there is an intimate relationship between a teacher's need for security and need for control.

Those who might look to me for advice on how to shed the need for control would do well to look elsewhere, for I could not begin to explain how one goes about doing this. I only know that it must begin with an identification of that need within oneself, followed by a growing understanding of how such a need relates to a sense of loss of personal power. This is a tricky admixture of personal-emotional stuff, and I believe that each of us has to sort this out in his or her own way. But I also believe that the need for personal power is a key emotional need in all of us. When that need is threatened, we tend to want to exert more control, which makes us feel safer and more secure. When the need for personal power is adequately fulfilled, it is easier to relinquish the need for control. That is quite a simple paradigm for a lifetime of serious self-study, for giving up behaviors that are no longer productive and replacing them with a new set of behaviors that are more in accord with one's educational values and with who we really want to be.

The very first time I became aware of how my controlling behaviors got in the way of students' thoughtful investigations was in Marti's class. The children in each of the science centers were busy carrying out their own experiments, following their own agendas. Feeling like a third wheel in the face of all this sciencing, I walked around from center to center, observing, and butting in my two cents' worth: "Hmmm, Trisha. Why do you think that is happening? Why don't you try that and see what happens?" I now cringe to see myself in this role—diverting children's attention from their inquiries and shifting their minds onto other, unrelated lines of investigation. I thought I was doing the "teacher's job," when, in fact, I was just getting in the way of children's own serious inquiries.

I will never forget the look on Darien's face when I said to him, "Why don't you try that and see how that works?" It was as if I had slapped him. Who WAS this woman, and why was she in my face? His look shamed me and gave me the first good look at my noble intentions, gone wrong. Could I leave children to their own inquiries in their investigative play? Would their inquiries be less, or more, productive if I did that? Could I save my interventions for the debriefing period, when I would get my chance to raise the questions that would further their thinking about the phenomena under investigation?

A long period of retreating from such intrusions allowed me to study what does happen when I don't interfere. Children and adult learners get on with their inquiries, and I do have a chance to use what I see as working material in the debriefing period. I do have a chance to study what the children are doing, and how they are doing it, and to make notes about their ability to conduct inquiries, to work together cooperatively, to pursue and test hypotheses, to solve problems. Investigative play is for the children's play. I have taught myself to step back from it and to allow it to happen. My need for control has been relinquished, and it is liberating.

BUT IS IT TEACHING?

I arrange a Play-Debrief-Replay activity around the topic of evaluation for a group of preservice teachers in the professional development program at my university. It's taken me several days to design what I considered to be two investigative play tasks that address the big ideas of evaluation and that would open doors to inquiry about classroom practice. The students work in cooperative-learning groups on the first task, and my observations tell me that they are seriously engaged. The discussions are intense; issues are

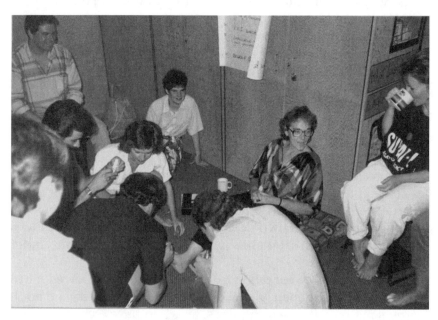

But is it teaching?

being examined from several different perspectives; implications for classroom practice are suggested. I am satisfied that the play task is working. I continue to walk from group to group, keeping my distance so that my presence is not intrusive but staying close enough to tune in to what is being said. I carry my coffee cup with me and take sips while studying the room.

Debriefing is rich, productive, and thoughtful. Issues are examined, and provocative questions carry the discussion to new levels of inquiry. It has been satisfying for me to see that the tasks I designed have done the job. When the discussion on evaluation has been exhausted, I shift gears, asking the students to observe the nature of the process.

"And what about the teacher's role? What did you observe about that?"

"Well," says Ivan, "you were walking around the room, drinking coffee, watching us."

"Was I teaching?" I ask him, throwing him a curve.

He is stuck, thinks, then responds with uncertainty, "Yes."

I feign alarm. "So I'm walking around the room, drinking coffee, and you call that teaching?"

Ivan is nonplused, thinking hard. He is more uncertain. "Yes," he says. "I call that teaching."

Two years later, he comes to visit and tells me, "I still call that teaching."

(11)

Learning to Reflect on Practice

Highly competent teachers are thoughtful, intelligent observers of what goes on in the classroom. They are able to size up and make sense of complex situations and risk self-initiated actions that seem appropriate to the situation. In their problem-solving behaviors, they are able to watch themselves and apprehend the impact of their actions on the situation. This they do nondefensively, with an open attitude that allows for accurate assessment of their action. For these teachers, teaching is an "examined act," and in their ability to take risks to deal with problems creatively, they elevate teaching to an art.

M Y INTRODUCTION to case method teaching came out of the blue via a letter from C. Roland Christensen, then Robert Walmsley University Professor at Harvard University's Graduate School of Business. Thus began a long-standing friendship and collegial association and an opening of new doors in my approach to thinking and teaching.

In April 1986, the B-school hosted its 75th anniversary of teaching by the case method, offering an invitational seminar for 75 academics from around the world. Would I be interested in attending? What fool turns down an invitation to Harvard? Never mind that I came from a faculty of education and was being initiated into a group of professors of business, management, marketing, and economics. Never mind that I felt about as comfortable as a turkey on the day before Thanksgiving. I packed my leather suit, silk blouse, and black pumps and made myself ready for the hallowed halls of ivy.

It is claimed that case method teaching was born and bred at the Harvard Business School. Used there for more than 80 years, the methodology has "revolutionized management education all over the globe" (Ewing, 1991). Most business schools throughout North America and abroad have adopted case method teaching, and most of them use the cases written at Harvard and made available from Harvard's Case Clearinghouse. The reputation of the methodology to influence the thinking and behavior of students as business leaders is legion. The quality of discussion and analysis during study groups and whole-class discussions is cited as the means through which students begin to understand—truly understand—the complexities of doing business as well as develop their skills as seasoned thinkers and problem solvers.

WELCOME TO HARVARD!

Under the direction of Professor Christensen and his colleagues, we participants were immersed in 3 days of case method teaching. We became the students. But instead of studying business cases, we studied "teaching cases," those that had relevance to our professional domain. From these lived experiences, I began to understand how teaching with cases was a perfect fit with my own theoretical advocacy of "teaching for thinking." Cases were the "thinking activities" that promoted students' thoughtful examination of big ideas. Study questions, framed in higher order mode, elevated awareness of complex issues. Learned habits of observation and analysis led to informed decision making. There were no hard-and-fast answers; there were no certainties. The nature of the whole-class discussions that followed our study-group work was a manifestation of a teaching-for-thinking debriefing. Listening, reading, participating, and discussing in this hothouse environment, I felt that I had come home. Case teaching fit me like my old, comfortable shoes.

At the end of each day, we were wined and dined at the business school faculty club. I couldn't believe the luxury of it all—from the mile-long Oriental carpets, to the stacks of the *New York Times* and *Wall Street Journal* available for the taking, to the silver samovars of coffee and tea, always hot, to the lobster and steak dinners—this was life at the Business School. I felt like Cinderella at the ball, in a constant state of dis-ease. I did not belong in this land of abundance. But, my, was it ever a trip!

The steak and lobster dinners were a minor diversion. After dinner, we were expected to retreat to our study groups and begin our preliminary discussions about the cases that were to be taught the next day. In a very short time, we grew to know one another well, to count on one another's strengths, backgrounds of experience, and insights, as we climbed through the complex cases and wrestled with big ideas. We debated heatedly over proposed plans of action and readied ourselves with notes to enter the discussion arena the following day.

Praying that I would not be called on to "present the case for the morning," my throat dry, my eyes fatigued from lack of sleep, I watched the discussion leader open the session and call on a participant to summarize the case. This "cold call" kept all of us on our toes, ready to do our stuff if necessary yet enormously relieved when it was someone else's turn. But as the discussion heated up, each of us eagerly vied for airtime, hoping to give voice to what we believed was an informed perspective on the question.

Throughout my ordeal, sitting high up in the stadium seats that were designed for discussion teaching, I watched with awe as Professor Christensen conducted the case discussion. *Artist* is the word that immediately springs to mind. His skill in drawing out our ideas, his sharpness in knowing just the right questions to ask, his ability to extend thinking about an issue, reaching inside our heads to plumb the depths of our thinking, were masterful. He did all this in what appeared to be an effortless manner; when I knew him better, I realized how much energy it took from him. Revered by his students, acclaimed in a university that collected "stars" in every academic area, "Chris" was the exemplar of the case method. THIS was teaching!

Christensen had a passion for teaching that was palpable, and his energy and his passion infected us. His belief that successful teachers are not born, but made, gave direction to his life, as he continued to help teachers learn the art of discussion teaching and increase their power to affect students in profound ways.

I left the 75th-anniversary invitational seminar with a fire in the belly for case method teaching that has never left me. Oh, beware of converts!

A CASE FOR SOCIAL STUDIES

Several months later, Cathy Elliott, then assistant principal of Centennial Secondary School, telephoned to ask if I would be interested in doing some staff development with teachers at her school. I jumped at the chance, eager to see if teaching with cases could work in the secondary school. The curriculum area of social studies seemed potentially rich ground for such work, and I could already envision the kinds of cases that could be written to illuminate historical issues. Could cases enable students to learn important concepts in social studies? Could cases enable them to acquire important information? Would students who studied cases become more involved in the affective aspects of history? Would work with cases improve students' abilities as informed decision makers? I wanted to see if cases used at the high school level would bring about the development of habits of thinking seen in graduates of the Harvard Business School.

Knowing there was a potential group of interested teachers, and with support and encouragement from the administration, I developed a program for two stages of staff development. The first stage would consist of a full semester of in-service training activities with social studies teachers. The second stage would involve a follow-up semester of in-class work with cases, during which time data would be gathered about what happened in the classrooms.

All 14 social studies teachers attended the introductory session. My orientation provided teachers with information about the project and the extent of staff development work that would be involved. Everyone at the meeting was given a copy of a training handbook detailing the program. The teachers listened to my pitch, flipped through the handbook, and raised questions.

"Case study? It's just one more technique to add to what you do in the classroom, isn't it?"

"Nope," I said. "It's a way of teaching. Not just an 'add on' when things need sprucing up."

The teachers' reactions betrayed their resistance. Dozens of dissenting questions and comments filled the air. This approach wouldn't work because

"Cases take too much time. With such in-depth treatment of issues, we won't be able to cover the curriculum."

"The students need us to give them the information."

"The students are not accustomed to working on their own. They depend on us to tell them what to do."

"The students don't know how to work responsibly in groups. They'll be off task, and we'll have a lot of behavior to deal with."

Where had I heard all that before—those same refrains that betray a lack of confidence in students' ability to think, to function, on their own? The resistance that comes with nonacceptance of the nonfamiliar? Factor into the equation the notion that such a pedagogy requires teachers to relinquish some of their control and give it over to students. At the high school level, no less! Blasphemy!

The staff development program I was offering definitely stirred the juices. The teachers responded with a barrage of seemingly legitimate caveats about why this wouldn't work. If, however, they could borrow a few cases to liven up existing teaching practices—well, that might be worth having. But me? Change my stuff? Not a chance!

I emphasized that participation in the program would be strictly voluntary. But in my heart, I knew that this was my way of letting teachers who were strong dissenters off the hook. I felt too old and tired to burden the program with classic resisters and nagging dissenters, who not only are *not* open to new ideas, but who inevitably take a toll on the emotional climate of the group and of the instructor.

At the second session, 2 weeks later, six teachers had already vanished into their own classrooms; yet there was still much resistance in the air. The remaining group of eight complained about the readings, about the degree of effectiveness of the methodology, about the competence of the students, about having to attend professional development sessions to learn the new strategies. The teachers "dissed" me, sharing in-jokes about their "bad" classes and students. How could I possibly know about the real world of the classroom? I responded to all comments, trying to keep a nonjudgmental tone, remaining respectful, working hard not to fall into a defensive posture. After the session was over, I had a bad headache.

Two weeks later, at the third session, five more teachers opted out, and we were down to a hard-core group of three. I tried not to be disappointed at the numbers, telling myself that these were the ones who really wanted to be there. During the afternoon, we were approached by a biology teacher, a journalism teacher, an ESL (English as a second language) teacher, and a humanities teacher, who asked if they might be permitted to join us. This group of seven remained together for the duration of the two semesters and, in fact, gave us the opportunity to see case method work in different subject areas. In that third session the training program took a serious step forward.

ANATOMY OF CASE METHOD TEACHING

Learning from the teachers at Centennial Secondary School, benefiting from their wisdom, insight, and risk taking, I eventually put my own spin on case method teaching, retooling the methodology to fit the less rarefied clientele of the secondary school. The "pure" form of the methodology I observed at the Harvard Business School was intended for sophisticated graduate students, who were carefully selected from an elite bunch of applicants. Most of them came with considerable experience in the business world. They didn't have to be motivated to learn. Their huge tuition fees were motivation enough for them to be serious students. Without exception, they all were hungry to become the new masters of the business universe. The world of teaching and learning at Harvard couldn't have been more different from the world of the high school student.

As I worked to reconceptualize the applications of case method for secondary school students, I needed to ensure that the principles of case method teaching remained inviolate. If case method was going to deliver on its promise of teaching students to communicate their ideas more effectively, examine complicated issues in more critical ways, make informed decisions based on data, and become more curious and more interested in learning, respect different views, attitudes, and beliefs, and become more motivated to read material beyond that presented in class, the principles must remain uncorrupted. Within a wide spectrum of variations and individual applications, it was not difficult for the Centennial teachers to make certain that the key ingredients of case method teaching—cases, study questions, study groups, whole-class debriefing, and follow-up activities—be the core of their classroom work.

From the very beginning, we needed to create a resource of cases—those remarkable teaching tools that are framed in narrative voices around certain "big ideas"—the issues in the curriculum that warrant serious, in-depth examination. We spent much of the first semester writing cases, and we eventually created a publication of 20 cases for secondary school classes (Bickerton et al., 1991).

Cases needed to come with a list of study questions that provoke thoughtful examination of the issues in the case, and the Centennial teachers were learning more new skills: how to phrase questions that were in the "higher order" categories; how to avoid questions that had single, fact-based answers; how to avoid the empty "why" questions; how to avoid leading questions. It was a toss-up with respect to who was learning more in these sessions, the teachers or me. Teaching as learning.

In our little group of seven, I taught a case and debriefed it, demonstrating the interaction skills that I had known from my earlier work with Play-Debrief-Replay activities and that I had seen modeled by Chris at Harvard. Analysis of the debriefing allowed the teachers to study critically what I had done as well as their own responses to the interactive dialogue. They became "students," as I had been at the business school.

Would I now teach one of their cases with real students? Would I take on one of their social studies classes and show them how it worked in classroom practice? Yikes! Talk about cold calls! Was I ready for this? Unsure of my own skills and unfamiliar with the students, I persuaded myself that this was important—for me, and for our group. Sure, I would do it. Steve Fukui and Rich Chambers had written "The Case of Injustice in Our Time," about the internment of ethnic Japanese during World War II, and they asked if I would teach it.

Steve let me take over his class. It was arranged that the session would be videotaped, so that we could study it afterward—dissect it and learn from what happened. I felt like a novice skier, racing down the slopes at 90 miles an hour, trying to remember the ski instructor's advice: Don't panic!

My case study colleagues filed into the classroom. The video equipment was rolled in by the audiovisual technician and set up in the rear. All those people! The camera on me! The students had generously agreed to this three-ring circus, happy as would be so many students, for a break in the normal routine of the class day. They had read the case (or so they said) in advance and had spent the past 30 minutes in study groups prior to this debriefing. Of course, none of these students had had any prior experience with cases. So we were all virgins.

My hubris at thinking that I could do this is astonishing to me now. I had seen it done and had conducted many debriefings of "plays" in a similar fashion, but I had never actually taught a case. Yet I was teaching others how to do it. If this was going to be my comeuppance, then it was surely deserved.

I was determined NOT to begin the case with a cold call; I didn't believe in it and saw it as disrespectful to the students with whom I was working. Instead, I began by asking the kind of introductory question that would set the case in context.

"What do you see as the key issues in this case?"

The silence was mind-numbing, and I caught Steve and Rich giving each other sly smiles. Been there, done that.

I waited. The silence was now profound.

I waited.

A boy near the front finally, finally, raised his hand and said, "I think it's about how they treated the Japanese, and it was unfair."

The sigh of relief that someone had actually responded must have been audible. I proceeded to react to the student, in what I thought would be the most safe, facilitative way: reflecting what he had said.

So I played his idea back. "You think the case is about the way the Japanese were treated, and you think that was unfair."

I was not prepared for his outburst.

"What's the matter with you? Are you deaf? That's what I said! Are you trying to make me sound like an idiot?"

I faltered. I apologized. Where had I gone wrong?

He wasn't finished with me. "I thought it was the teacher's job to make us feel good about ourselves, not make us feel stupid!"

How is it possible to be nondefensive in such a situation? I'm sure I blushed. I'm sure I stammered, looking for the right words.

The videotape kept rolling. I apologized again and asked for other comments. Would anyone else be brave enough to risk sharing his or her ideas after that?

I limped along through the rest of the debriefing, a sad excuse for a case study teacher.

Steve and Rich tried to comfort me after the session. They chuckled at my minor disaster, and although they were gracious enough to excuse what had happened by blaming it on a "difficult" student, I was not to be assuaged. We had all learned a big lesson: conducting a case discussion with a group of real students is much harder than it looks. We would all have to learn, by practice and reflection on action and from the encouragement of our support group, to continue to take risks on the growth pathway.

TEACHING WITH CASES

It's a warm September morning, and it's hard for the students to settle into the rhythm of school after the long summer vacation. They linger in the corridors in thick clusters, laughing, comparing schedules, giving advice, smooching. I worm my way down the hall, taking the pulse of the school. It feels warm, inviting. The ambiance is informal, casual; the ethnic mix diverse; the range of socioeconomic classes wide.

I've come to visit Rich Chambers's class in this, the second semester of our professional development work with case method teaching. Rich is going to teach his first case in his Grade 11 social studies class. I find what I think is an unobtrusive seat at the far side of the classroom, collecting shy glances from self-conscious 17-year-olds who oscillate between adolescence and emerging adulthood, as if caught in an out-of-control revolving door.

At the front of the room, Rich seems at ease, friendly, smiling. He reads aloud, as required, the announcements for the day: lasagna, green salad, and apple cake for lunch; team practice after school; parents' night in 2 weeks. I think about how curious a teacher's job is, with all these extraneous duties, and how gracefully such noninstructional demands are met.

Rich begins the real work by assigning students to small study groups of four students each. For now, he retains control of who is to work with whom. Later on, he will be able to shift gears and allow students to choose for themselves. In preparation for today's session, the students have been asked to read "A Case of Injustice in Our Time," the case I had attempted to teach with Steve's class the previous semester.

Rich's directions to the class are brief. The groups are to discuss the study questions on the last page of the case, observing two fundamental rules: (a) All students have the right to express their own ideas, and (b) all students' ideas are to be heard and treated respectfully. He has initiated such rules—and I am learning that, especially at the onset, students need to be reminded about the protocols for effective small-group discussion. These are learned skills and they don't magically appear when students are asked to form groups.

I ask the group near my chair if I may sit in with them. They shrug in indifferent assent.

The four students in "my" group—Mark, Steve, Taryn, and Carla—lay the sheet with the five study questions out in front of them. Taryn assumes leadership, vocalizing the first question: What hypotheses can you suggest that might explain the treatment of ethnic Japanese during World War II? Mark shuffles through his notebook. Steve and Carla are quiet, uncertain. Taryn repeats the question and presses them. "Didn't you guys read the case? I'll bet you didn't read the case."

Mark says defensively, "I read it."

Steve and Carla nod in agreement.

Then Taryn says, "So what do you think?"

The discussion begins to come alive. Mark is an active participant and takes the position that the Japanese got what they deserved. "After all," he asserts, with an air of one who knows the truth and is disgusted by those who don't see it his way, "they bombed Pearl Harbor." Steve, although less vocal, is clearly Mark's ally.

Taryn argues vehemently in opposition. She reminds them that Pearl Harbor is in the United States, and *not* in Canada, and she asks, "What did that have to do with us?" But Mark shrugs this off. "Canada and the U.S.—it's the same," he says to Taryn's raised eyebrows. He adds, "The Japanese in Canada were spies anyway, who would betray secrets to Japan, and that is why they had to be taken away."

I see Taryn growing more incensed with Mark's close-minded, made-in-Hollywood arguments. To her credit, she tries to stay calm, presenting data to refute Mark's points. She points out that these people of Japanese ethnicity were Canadian citizens, that they were being "convicted" without due process, and that their actual ties to Japan were, in many cases, remote. She also cites the fact that Germans in Canada, despite German aggression in Europe, were not subjected to the same treatment.

Mark and Steve are unyielding. They have made up their minds. "The Germans, after all, did *not* bomb Pearl Harbor," they say with authority, as if this explains everything. They are both locked, with dogmatic insistence, into a set of beliefs that they will not allow to be penetrated by the light of data.

The two boys and two girls are similarly split on the rest of the study questions. The longer the discussion continues, the more the prejudicial attitudes of these two boys are revealed and the more Taryn is astonished by their closed-mindedness. Carla, siding with Taryn, may lack the personal power, the verbal skills, or the thinking capabilities to take on her share of the debate; in any event, her support is largely nonverbal. Forty minutes melt away like ice cream on the Fourth of July. I am so taken up by the debate in "my" group that I have forgotten to tune in to any of the other group discussions. When the teacher calls time, I vaguely recall, the room has been abuzz.

Rich has allocated 40 minutes for study-group work and 40 minutes for debriefing. In this school, happily, the classes are 90 minutes long. Before beginning the debriefing session, he reminds the class of the two discussion guidelines. Again, I think about what a teacher needs to do to keep the discussion civilized, and that Rich has all this teaching skill at his fingertips. This is his first case discussion ever, but he shows no signs of nervousness. It seems as if he has been doing this all his life.

Using the same study questions, he begins by inviting responses to the first. The students are geared up for it. The study groups have oiled the engine and they are ready to rock and roll. Arms wave as students vie for airtime, and very quickly, the discussion heats up. What I saw in my small study group is now unleashed in the whole class. There is a clear split between those students who share Mark and Steve's views and those who agree with Taryn and Carla, but I'm disturbed that the split is heavily weighted in support of Mark. Racist feelings, thinly veiled by the rationalization of "wartime necessity," are strong, ugly, and unacknowledged.

I watch Rich and observe how he is leading the discussion. He's on the mark! He doesn't admonish students when they are presenting ideas that are not supported by data. He doesn't *tell* them that they are wrong, or silly. He doesn't say that they have to change their attitudes. He is a master of restraint. He avoids lecturing. He listens to the students' ideas thoughtfully, respectfully paraphrasing in a way that zeroes in on the significant issues so that the ideas are played back in a richer, more focused way. This he does without rewarding an idea as "good" or condemning it as "without value." The room begins to feel like a pressure cooker, yet the guidelines for discussion are consistently observed. There is considerable respect shown for this teacher; I believe that his reputation in this school, and with these students, has earned him that standing.

I note that more and more students are asking for airtime, and that participation is close to 100%. Rich has orchestrated the discussion so that students are free to say anything they think, without being judged.

Yoshimi, who has been a key player in the whole-class discussion, is now showing a deep distress over what her classmates have revealed. When she next gets her turn to speak, she ventures into dangerous waters. "I'm getting the terrible feeling . . . " She looks down at her shoes, then continues, "That if this were happening today—if the police came to my home and took my parents and me away like that—none of you . . . " She looks up, her eyes filling as she finishes her sentence. "Would stand up for me."

Everyone now begins to talk at once, as Yoshimi, shoulders bent, tries to keep the tears back. My own eyes fill, and I am humbled by the courage of this small, slight girl.

No one has noticed that the class is over. (No bells ring in this school.) No one leaves. Rich shouts directions now about the next class—the discussion will continue. A few students pack up and head for the door. Several cluster around Yoshimi. Rich works his way over to them. There is more they want to say, for they are angry, hurt. Yoshimi is also worried that she has gone too far. Will this mean she will lose some friends?

Rich, who is as overwhelmed as the students by what has occurred, continues to maintain his neutrality while at the same time offering reassurance. He explicitly praises the students' participation and applauds them for standing up for what they believe. The girls need a late pass for their next class.

When they are all gone, Rich turns to me and says, "I've been teaching social studies for 12 years, and I've never had an experience like this. This is what social studies should be about! But, boy, do I have a lot of work to do with this class!"

A week later, when Rich and I talk again, he tells me that the discussion on the case continued for two more class sessions and that there were many threads to be followed up. Follow-up activities have been suggested, and students are choosing to pursue studies on government and the law, propaganda in time of war, World War II, the War Measures Act. Follow-up readings are suggested, among them Joy Kogawa's *Obasan*, and the film *Come to the Paradise* is shown in a subsequent class.

By the time Rich teaches his second case, "Let's Have a War! That's a Good Idea!" written by his colleague Joe Gluska, he is already feeling his strength as a case study teacher. I, the learner, suck up all the details from my observations and discussions with students and teachers and continue to construct my own case study frameworks.

REFLECTIONS ON SELF IN THE PROCESS OF CASE TEACHING

From my own beginnings with teaching for thinking, I now marched headfirst into case method teaching. Early teaching experiences debriefing "plays" were my advance organizers, and I rounded off many rough edges in my thinking and practice from my work with the Centennial Case Study Project teachers, my initial experiences at the Harvard Business School, my continued readings in the area, and my ongoing dialogue with Chris Christensen. All these building blocks shaped my thinking and practice. But what made much of the growth possible were the degrees of freedom I was given at my university to take what I knew into classrooms, use cases in my classes, and observe, from reflection *in* and *on* action, what I was doing and what I needed to do to improve. Watching myself on video playback was always an ordeal, but an invaluable opportunity to reexamine practice in the aftermath of the case discussion.

Practice and self-scrutiny are the meat and potatoes of the growth process; all the other stuff is appetizer. Little by little, in painful half-inch steps, I was teaching myself to become a case teacher.

After teaching dozens of cases, and after writing dozens of cases, I discover that there is a hierarchical order to the study questions. Why hadn't I seen that before? I now understand that instead of throwing higher order questions at students helter skelter, it is more productive to begin with data-gathering questions then move on to questions that call for analysis, then to questions that ask that values be identified, and then to questions that call for evaluative judgments and only after that to calls for plans of action. I never clued into this in the Harvard sessions—I was too busy being a part of it, focused on the whole and not seeing the elegant intricacies of how the discussion evolved.

I find a vital piece of help in an article by Adena Rosmarin, "The Art of Leading a Discussion" (1985). When I read it, I know that this is the missing link, the piece that I'd been looking for that completes the picture and makes it whole. I see that what is good can now become elegant, better focused. I hypothesize that students who are put through such a process again and again in their case discussions will become accustomed to applying such habits of thinking to problem solving: gathering and analyzing data, identifying value positions, evaluating options, and, only then, moving to action. Wouldn't it be wonderful if problems could be examined first, by data gathering, and only later one would move to action? In my experience, even with adult academics the tendency is to begin problem solving with action plans. Never mind the other stuff.

A faculty colleague, Tom O'Shea, invites me to take his math education class. He is going off to attend a conference and needs someone to fill in for him. I jump at the chance of teaching the case "It's Up to You, Mrs. Buscemi"—a case that I have written but never taught—to a group of preservice math teachers (Wassermann, 1993, pp. 156–160).

The students straggle in like mournful souls from a lost weekend and find seats around the small tables. It's a rainy Monday morning in Education 475, Designs for Learning: Mathematics. The students come prepared to examine the issue of evaluation practices in mathematics.

Laura Bickerton, one of the teachers from the Centennial Case Study Project group, asks if she might sit in. I know she is studying me the way I studied Chris—but she forgets that I've been learning alongside her. Chris conducts a case like Glenn Gould plays Bach. I see myself as Bertie Tenthumbs, playing "Chopsticks." Laura must pay a price for her visit: She will meet with me afterward, and help to debrief my discussion-teaching strategies. She is insightful and very smart, and I feel lucky to have her feedback.

The students have read the case, and we begin with a brief introduction to the session, followed by small-group work on the case questions. I've prepared a different list of debriefing questions in advance, so that we are not going over exactly the same territory as was covered in the study groups, yet it is not so far removed that a priori thinking could not be used to construct new meanings. I've positioned the questions in the hierarchy that I've learned. I try to keep the list of questions down to seven, but even so, and even with 90 minutes allocated to discussion, I'm often unable to get at them all and have to make modifications while we are in process. If this should happen today, I will ask Laura for her suggestions about how I might have streamlined the discussion, and where she thinks I might have moved more quickly.

I always prepare a case the day before I am to teach it. This I do by rereading it carefully and underlining what I consider to be key issues that will be examined and highlighted in the discussion. At first, I found it strange that I vary the highlights for the same case, depending on the class. But later I understood why. As different students contribute to discussions, different aspects in the case are brought to light, and different perspectives emerge. I learn more about a case each time I teach it. This may sound funny, since most of the cases I teach are ones that I've written myself.

After reading and studying the case, I then prepare, in draft, my list of discussion questions, carefully framing them so that they invite open-ended discussion on the issues, ensuring that they are respectfully worded and clear in what they are asking to be examined. Each time I teach a case, I prepare the discussion questions anew, learning from what has gone before and orienting the questions toward the particular group. Questions for experienced teachers may have a different slant from those for a group of sophomores, who have yet to begin professional training. These acts of studying the cases again and again and of learning to frame questions that are appropriate to different groups and that highlight important aspects of the case continue to inform my practice and allow me to hone my skills. I would no more consider going into a case discussion without this extensive preparation than I would going in with my knickers down.

The case of Mrs. Buscemi is one of my favorites. It's based on a situation that was related to me by a colleague who teaches in a New York City public high school. I promised to keep her name out of it—but I want her to know that I'm very grateful to her for allowing me access to this story. The case involves several related issues that bear on educational practice. On the surface, it presents a situation in which a teacher is faced with the dilemma of whether to fail Adam, a student in her Grade 12 math class. This failure would mean that the student would not be able to graduate. There are more complex issues. Adam Wright, a minority student from an impoverished family, has been promised a scholarship to a junior college, contingent on the successful completion of his 12th year. Mrs. Buscemi believes that Adam deserves to fail, because his work has not measured up to her standards. She has determined Adam's final grade by totaling his five test scores, his classroom participation, and his homework, and then dividing the sum by 7. She has rounded off the average mark of 43%, in Adam's favor, to 45%.

The principal argues Adam's case with Mrs. Buscemi. Wouldn't Mrs. B. give this young man a chance for a better future by allowing him to pass? After all, Adam wasn't shirking; he's a nice boy who, because of his part-time job, his after-school preparatory classes, and his other courses, simply was unable to put the extra effort needed into his math work. The principal tells Mrs. B., "This would be the very first person in Adam's family who ever had a chance for higher education." How could Mrs. Buscemi deny Adam that opportunity?

Since Tom O'Shea has asked me to focus on evaluative practices in math, the questions I write require an examination of Violet Buscemi's teaching practices, her effectiveness in providing help for Adam, the procedures she used in making her evaluative judgments of his work, the student and his performance, and the role of the principal. Issues of affirmative action and fairness and accuracy in evaluation practices are pivotal. The final question I write has to do with action: What would these students do in Violet Buscemi's place?

The students divide themselves into five study groups and within minutes are deeply engaged with the study questions. I observe and listen from the sidelines. I have learned not to sit with any group: Experience has taught me that when I join in, students inevitably begin to "play to me"—looking at my face to "read" it for signs of whether they are coming up with the "right answers." From the sidelines, however, I make mental notes about the nature and extent of participation of individual students and how the groups are digging into the examination of the issues.

It is not a surprise to me that there is a wide spectrum of difference in ideas about the issues and the way they are perceived. From reading the same case, students have all sorts of different perspectives about the teacher, the student, and the principal—it's as if they had been reading different cases. This is important working material for me; I learn that participants in case discussion filter data through their own perceptual screens, so that no data are "truths." By the time the data get processed in each mind, they come out as different views. We take in data "from where we sit on the medicine wheel," as a Native American friend once put it, and this has been a valuable lesson. The study groups are tremendously valuable, since this is the first "screening" of the issues and it allows students to hear points of view markedly different from their own.

When the allocated study-group time is nearly up, I take a sign around the room, indicating that there are 5 minutes left until the groups will come together for the debriefing. I use this quiet signal because it is less intrusive than shouting over the clamor of voices or attempting another kind of disrespectful interruption. At the end of the study session period, groups are still arguing; there's rarely any closure in case discussion. In fact, from experience I know that long after a case has been taught, students continue to process their ideas about it. Cases are like onions that are being continually peeled, and with each new layer comes new awareness, new understandings. A student once told me that a case she had studied several years earlier was still "playing out in her head. What's more," she added, "I think that I'll be thinking about it for the next dozen years." I wonder what other instructional tool has such power.

As the study groups shift chairs and mindsets, getting ready for whole-class discussion, I steal a quick look at my list of discussion questions—one last review before I take on the big task of discussion teaching. I wait until the students are settled, then I give them the discussion guidelines: Raise hands when you want to offer an idea; be prepared to engage with me, over perhaps two or three interchanges; feel free to tell me to "back off" if you think you want to be let off the hook and have me go on to another person.

I begin with the data-gathering question: "I'd like to start by asking you to give me some data about the key players in this case: Violet Buscemi and Adam Wright. But before you give me your ideas, please try, insofar as you are able, to stay with data, and reserve opinions, judgments, and attributions, for a later question."

There is a flurry of hands, and at once the discussion takes off. There is no dearth of willing participants; no backbenchers in this group. Nearly everyone wants to speak.

Orchestrating a case discussion—making sure that I don't call on the same people all the time, making sure that my peripheral vision takes in the whole group and not just one side of the room, making sure that before I move on to a subsequent question I've given everyone a chance to have his or her ideas expressed—all these "discussion management" skills are also in play. Being respectful and showing that respect to all in the group is a sine qua non—that guides my tone of voice and the way the questions are put.

We work first with the data, and we begin to draw a profile of Violet, another one of Adam. Sean offers an opinion: "I think that Violet feels that she has to obey the principal's order because she feels vulnerable as a new teacher." I ask Sean if he is able to rephrase his opinion statement as a data statement subtly reminding him that we are still gathering data and avoiding judgments and assumptions. He thinks for a few moments and then says, "She is a new teacher." I suggest that perhaps he wants to save the other parts of his statement for a later question, when we examine hypotheses.

After each student's statement, I have several choices to make in my response. Do I paraphrase and play back what she or he has said? Do I merely accept, with thanks, the contribution? Do I ask that further analysis be made, that examples be given, that supporting data be provided? Do I challenge the student to think beyond what has been offered? As I reflect on my choices, I consider the effect of my response, where it will take the course of the discussion, as well as how it will further the student's thinking about the issues. All this is done in the mind, in a fraction of an instant; there are no wrong choices, though there may be choices that torque the discussion and shift it onto another pathway, that create a challenge too soon in the process, that don't do enough to promote further reflection. I study my response and its effect on the student and on the pathway of the discussion, trying to hold back my self-criticism when I believe I should have done something differently. All this is playing in my head like a Puccini opera—thousands of notes in counterpoint that I am trying to keep harmonic and prevent from becoming a cacophony.

Jennie puts her hand up and begins to speak before I have had a chance to "finish" with Sean. I look at her and tell her that I know she is anxious to "get in there," but I'm going to "put her on hold" and will get back to her once I'm sure that Sean has said all he wants to say. Sean tells me that he is now finished, and I remember to get back to Jennie, thanking her for waiting. This is another way of managing the discussion, asking students to respect others' turns and remembering to get back to them once I've told them that I would. I've got a lot of balls juggling in the air, and keeping them all up there and not dropping any takes a lot of concentration. It is much more difficult than giving a lecture about affirmative action or the vulnerability of new teachers. But as I watch myself in action, I get a sense of my growing skills, and when the discussion is focused, moving smoothly, I smile inwardly, pleased with how far I've come. Zen and the art of case teaching?

When we've drawn the profiles of Violet and Adam, I shift gears and begin questioning on the level of data analysis: "What hypotheses can you come up with that might explain Adam's poor performance in math?"

The question subtly requires students to consider several reasons for a student's poor performance, to examine possibilities, to get away from simple and simplistic judgments, such as "He's just lazy." In framing my questions, I keep in mind that I'm trying to build habits of thinking that will endure as these preservice teachers enter the world of the schools.

When many hypotheses are offered and further examined in terms of their credibility, I shift gears again and ask the question that relates to making judgments about evaluative practices. I try to be neutral in my tone: "So tell me, what is your 'take' on Violet's methods of evaluating Adam's work and of determining his final grade?" If I want open and honest responses, if I want students to "think their own thoughts," I must not betray any of my own thinking about Violet's practices in this case. My question sets up a thunderstorm of argument—and this is not a surprise. The issues in and around evaluation are tense, and much personal experience is read into what Violet did. I have a hard time getting to everyone who wants to speak; the time is running out fast, and I want to get to the last two questions before we have to end the session. When I am conducting a case discussion, I seem always to be at war with the clock, always having to make quick decisions about which course of action to pursue, what to omit, what to include, what to sacrifice, what to save.

I decide it's more important to shift gears, move to the value question, leave time for the action question, and thus sacrifice giving students second turns to speak. "So, where do you stand on the issue of affirmative action? Should students like Adam get a leg up in situations like these?" It's as if I had uncorked a hurricane from a bottle. I feel like a driver with a team of horses, each wanting to go in a different direction. Managing the discussion is becoming more difficult. Issues in and around evaluative practices are always full of passion.

With 10 minutes left, I shift to the last question. "What should Violet do?" I ask the students to consider all the data that have been shared, as well as the analyses, the judgments, and the value positions, in making their suggestions. There are, of course, many different views, and several of them seem credible to me. I throw them the last curve: "Which is the best plan? What values does it protect? And how do you know it's the best?" I leave them with that so that it may reverberate, or "cook," for a while. The lack of closure is unsettling; people want to continue talking, and many will do so after class, at lunch, and driving home in their shared rides. A good case is never finished.

AT HOME WITH UNCERTAINTY

As I've told my students many times, "There's no free lunch." Often with each blessing comes a price. I am teaching myself to be a case teacher, but there are things I have had to give up in order to be more successful at this way of being with students.

I've seen that I can no longer—never again—play the role of teacher-guru that is so much a part of the academic life. (Isn't this what professors do? Isn't this what students expect their professors to do?) This role I have now shed, like my academic robes at the end of commencement exercises. Case method teaching requires that my students are my partners in learning; in a case discussion, the partners are seeking to put ideas and issues under examination, and the playing field is level. No one has the "right" answers.

I've had to take further steps in relinquishing control—giant steps now, with no wish to return to safer ground. Giving control over to students to offer their ideas in a climate that is free from judgment is no longer hard to do. For one who began her teaching life with the view that the control of every aspect of teaching and learning was everything, this is a sea change. While I stepped lightly at first, as though skating on very thin ice, I have grown to love the liberty of it.

I've become comfortable with the ambiguities and uncertainties of cases with no correct answers; I am now easily able to leave the discussion open, to allow ideas to simmer, to avoid any kind of closure that will bring thinking to a halt. Leaving it alone, and letting the students work their own way out of the muddle of what they believe—that's no longer so tough.

More important, I no longer feel that I have the right to tell students what to think. I now believe that doing so would be an abrogation of my primary duty as a teacher, which is to build students' strengths as thinkers and problem solvers.

Laura comes to visit me and tells me about a problem situation in her school. I listen and we both begin to laugh. "It's a case," she says. "It's funny how I see the world in cases." This is our strength and our Achilles heel, since there doesn't seem any going back.

Providing Evaluative Feedback That Is Enabling

Highly competent teachers use many different kinds of evaluation procedures, depending on what is appropriate and what is purposeful. The methods of evaluation do not in any way diminish the dignity of the student. Evaluations include suggestions for improvement, and these are communicated to the students.

W HEN I WAS a student in fourth grade, I received my most stinging rebuke from a teacher, a comment so hurtful and vile that I have suffered its effect since that time. Our class was to give a play about colonial times in America, and I desperately wanted to be chosen for a part. When all the parts had been given out, and I had still not been selected, I thought I was finished—but no. There was the part of the announcer. Would I be able to do that? Did I have the proper white blouse and pleated skirt that was required? I assured my teacher on both questions, bending the truth without conscience. Under the kind of pressure only a 9-year-old can exert, my mother purchased the white blouse and navy skirt for me that evening, taking money desperately needed elsewhere for my school costume. I had no trouble memorizing my lines, and I was prepared and ready to perform by the time of the first rehearsal.

Our class was seated quietly, as became aspiring actors, in the large auditorium of PS 174, with its motto etched in scripted font over the top of the stage: DO UNTO OTHERS AS YOU WOULD HAVE OTHERS DO UNTO YOU. Pridefully sporting my white blouse, red tie, and pleated skirt, I was called to the stage to make the announcement that the play was to begin. In my enthusiasm, I raced up to the platform, tripping on the stair, falling flat on my face, pleated skirt flying up around my shoulders, knickers and bum exposed to the light of the midmorning sun. Every one of my classmates, all audience to this calamity, snickered at this gaffe of monumental proportions.

Before I had even got to my feet, the teacher was at my side, her fury out of control. The names she used to dress me down ring in my ears still—*fat, clumsy, stupid*. How could I have a part in the play? I would be an embarrassment to her and the whole class. I returned to my seat, consumed with shame.

Was it this painful event in my life that taught me about the effect of hurtful criticism on the ego and the feelings of self-worth of a child? Perhaps this experience was not my only teacher, but I promise you that since that day I have never ever been able to stand up in front of a group without feeling an enormous surge of anxiety—would I fall on my face this time? Would I once again be subject to the teacher's rebukes? Do we ever get over such an emotional assault?

REVISITING EVALUATION PRACTICES

What? Another chapter on evaluation practices? Haven't I said quite enough in Chapter 7 about this onerous task of teachers? Maybe this is more than anyone wants to know, but I can't quite finish the topic of evaluation until I have addressed the quite different issues of learning to use evaluative feedback that is respectful, that protects the dignity of students, that deepens students' understanding about their work, and that provides the stepping stones for their continued growth.

My initial work in marking and grading students' work was, like the rest of my teaching, inept. There was nothing in my teacher-training program that even broached the subject of evaluative feedback; it was as if it was so insignificant, it was not worthy of mention.

We did learn, of course, about standardized testing and the meanings of validity and reliability—questions posed and answered on final exams but utterly useless for classroom practice. So for me, this important aspect of teaching was a product of what I learned as a student at the hands of my own teachers. What was wrong with that? I'd survived 12-plus years of it, hadn't I? And who, in those days when dinosaurs roamed the earth, ever considered the negative effects of evaluation on the hearts and minds of learners? (How many do today?) I'm sure there were some teachers who believed that, like strapping, punitive criticism was just what children needed to "whip them into shape." Although some adults may still cling to such beliefs, it is happy news that most teachers have abandoned such malicious views along with the district-issued strap.

With worksheets that called for single, right answers, it was an easy job to tick off the "rights" and "wrongs" with checks and exes, tally up the results and put a mark on the top of a paper. That seemed reasonable and fair. Evaluation as a judging-and-grading process— never as a process to further student inquiry. A worksheet exercise, or a test, was a performance to be critically assessed, not a learning experience.

It was only when I returned from a year of graduate work to teach sixth grade at the Lee Road School, and began to initiate "thinking activities" into the curriculum, that I was confronted with the need for a different manner of evaluative feedback. Making comparisons, writing summaries, observing phenomena, classifying and interpreting data, examining assumptions—all these activities that students were asked to do and that are based on higher order thinking operations begged for different evaluative responses. There was just no way to tally thinking tasks with checks and eckses. I had to read and respond accordingly to the quality of *thinking*. In response to students' work on their thinking activities I learned to write comments that came largely from my work with the thinking theory, first reflective, and then raising hopefully provocative questions to stimulate further thinking:

"I see, Eddie, that you have compared life in your town with the life of a boy in an African village, according to housing, education, and clothing. I'm wondering if you've made some assumptions here. Can you check your paper again and see if you have?"

"Mark, you've written that what happened in the schoolyard was 'not our fault.' Can you explain a bit more about what you mean by 'not our fault?'"

"Bob, can you see any differences between amphibians and reptiles?"

"Debbie, can you think of any possible ways in which that might work?"

Even so, my evaluative practices remained a mixed bag. I learned to write clarifying and provocative questions on students' thinking activities; but when it came to other work, I continued to use *good* and *excellent* and other such judgmental terms indicating my approval. Happily, I am able to recall that even in those early years, I did not respond punitively, such as in

You can do better than this!
No, that's not right!
You should have studied harder!
This is just not satisfactory.

Those kinds of "ouch" comments lay too close to the bone for me.

This emerging new mindset on evaluative feedback had at least two negative sides. First, it was incredibly time-consuming; with a class of 33 students, I was now spending a lot of after-school hours reading and commenting on their papers. Second, such nonjudgmental, facilitative feedback was far from appreciated by the students, who were habituated to judging and ranking. "How can I know how I'm doing, if you don't give me a mark?" was a not uncommon criticism. Teaching the children the reasons for abandoning the old system of grading and using facilitative comments instead was one more challenging task on my new learning pathway.

FACILITATIVE FEEDBACK

About 6 months after the windup of the two-semester staff development project in case method teaching described in Chapter 11, the three social studies teachers from the group asked to meet with me about some concerns they were having about evaluation.

"Case study teaching," Rich Chambers told me, "does not fit with the kinds of tests we have traditionally used to assess students' work."

"We need to have another means of evaluating students that is more in keeping with the case method," Joe suggested.

In educational circles, it has been said that "the test wags the curriculum." In this case, it was a matter of the curriculum demanding change in testing and marking procedures.

Developing Assessment Tools

This initial meeting eventually gave life to a collection of assessment tools, *Evaluation Practices for the Graduation Program* (Adam, Chambers, Fukui, Gluska, & Wassermann, 1991). In this resource, hundreds of evaluative tools requiring application of principles of knowledge, rather than recall of information, have been suggested for teachers who wish to consider alternatives to traditional single-, right-answer tests. The teachers who generated these tools took pains to ensure that they reflected a multi-intelligence approach to students' "showing their stuff." Every one of these tools flies in the face of the single-, correct-answer performance measure; every one demands qualitative feedback.

These teachers, new to case method teaching, and newer still to qualitative assessment, looked at the overwhelming task in front of them: students from their many sections, turning in assignments that required lengthy reading, comments, and final grades. How could they accomplish this and ensure that their families would not evict them for nonappearance? As we talked together about facilitating the marking and grading strategies, it became obvious that very clear criteria—performance standards—were necessary in making evaluative decisions. If the teachers were absolutely clear about what they were looking for, about what standards had to be fulfilled in a task, the job of qualitative assessment would be easier.

So performance criteria were included for each section of assessment tools. What's more, the performance criteria were to be made clear to students who were undertaking that particular assessment option. Of course, students were given choices with respect to which assessment tool they would use, in order to demonstrate competency.

Steve Fukui developed a grid for assigning the grades that were required by the school board and that would reflect a teacher's judgment about a student's performance on a particular task. It seemed very complicated to me, but the teachers understood it, and they seemed to think it was going to work. I wondered if, with all the work coming in for evaluation, and no shortcuts for checking and ticking right and wrong answers, the teachers would survive the end of semester evaluation ordeals. I was not prepared for what happened.

Steve said that it was true that there was more labor—but he found the work much more interesting and pleasurable. Looking at different students' projects, different ways of students' showing their stuff, was much more varied, more fun, and more enjoyable than the tedious, repetitive work of marking answers. In addition, not all the projects required reading; some were three-dimensional works of art, dioramas, scrapbooks, videotapes. What came into the teachers' offices was, Joe Gluska told me, beyond astonishing in terms of what the students could and did do. The teachers were overwhelmed with the results; and the students, never to be underestimated, showed themselves to be champions. Of course, all these evaluative measures demanded a different kind of feedback.

Some Guiding Principles

It starts with the curriculum task. A student essay is the most familiar form in which facilitative feedback is normally given for students to "grow on." I was able to use what I learned from the case-study-project teachers, and I began to design performance tasks for my own students that allowed them to show their stuff on a variety of learning dimensions related to my university courses. And I was to become very particular in identifying the performance criteria that had to be met for each task.

That, of course, was the merest beginning.

From my own hurtful experiences in school and from work with students over the years, I have learned that the evaluative comments of teachers have enormous power for students. Frequently, students hear these comments as truths about themselves, rather than as a teacher's opinions. A consequence for learners is that these evaluative judgments are often integrated into a student's beliefs about self. I know that if a student has heard again and again that her work is not good, of poor quality, failing, she is likely to grow to believe that not only her work, but she, too, is not good, of poor quality, and a failure. And I know full well the impact of such subtractive comments on the growing self and the extent to which students become encumbered by them and become "can't do" nonlearners. As I wrote in Chapter 5, punitive, hurtful feedback doesn't inspire children to do better; it defeats them and keeps them from trying.

> I know, too, the effects of such responses as:
> I can see that your story came from your heart. To me, it is real and alive. Thank you for letting me read it.
> Your work excites me! When you compared the old woman to the proud, timid Heron, it created such powerful images in my mind—I think I'll remember those images always.

Such positive feedback affects feelings about self, feelings about the subject, and later performance.

It's clear to me that evaluative feedback may work toward the enablement of student learning and may also work to diminish student learning. Evaluative comments in the hands of an unskilled or uncaring teacher may be hurtful, disabling, and life-crippling. In the hands of a skilled teacher, evaluative practices may inspire pupils to new heights of performance and guide them toward greater mastery of skills and love of subject.

In real practice, what a teacher does is truly a reflection of deeply held beliefs. If teachers truly and deeply believe that harshly critical comments directed at students are the key to enabling them as learners, I wonder what more I might say to disabuse them of such ideas. If teachers truly and deeply believe that students can and should be informed of their performance strengths and weaknesses, and that there are better and more helpful ways of doing this than simply telling them that their work is rubbish, then they are likely to move heaven and earth to find those ways. This may mean not only developing new evaluation strategies, but also defying conventional practice. The task is not to be taken lightly; the forces of human nature make us reluctant to give up behaviors that have become ingrained in the fabric of our lives, no matter how discrepant with logic they may be.

Stepping away from judging and punishing, and moving toward facilitative feedback requires a giant leap of belief and of learned skills.

It requires the ability to "listen" to your comments and "hear" the possible effects of them on the student who is going to read them the next day. It requires the ability to look into the heart of a student's paper, to find its true value, and to see what needs to be strengthened. This skill in diagnosis is also learned, and grows, with reflection and practice over time. It requires the ability to use specific performance criteria against which the students' work is assessed. It requires the ability to be fair and equitable in assessing all students' work against the same standards. It requires the ability to abandon forever those comments that are utterly useless: "Tighten your style!" "Good!" "Work harder!" It requires the ability to be absolutely truthful, to pull no punches, to never say something is "good" or "promising" or "a good effort" when in fact it is inadequate. It requires the ability to write evaluative comments that encompass all these parts and to phrase them in such a way that the student is encouraged, feels affirmed, and understands what he or she needs to do to improve.

Finally, it requires a degree of compassion for students, for whom much is riding on the evaluative feedback they are to receive. I have found that my ability to be compassionate erodes when I am too tired, too run down, too burned out, to evaluate thoughtfully. I have found that my ability to be compassionate slips from me when I have a particular grudge against a student who has, for example, been consistently late to class. I am best at giving fair, equitable, helpful, compassionate feedback when I am fresh and when I can free myself from any negative prejudgments about a student when reading his or her paper. But whoever said it was easy?

EVALUATION WITHOUT TEARS

I long ago abandoned red-penning students' papers. I read ominous warnings into the color red. When I write comments on students' papers, I use lead pencil, for one important reason: I want to give myself the option of erasing something I have written after I've finished writing it, after I've read and reconsidered what I've written. Like any good editor, I want the chance to revise my comments. I generally write quickly, scribbling down my thoughts in handwriting that can only be described as atrocious. But I want to get all the thoughts down fast—everything I want to say! So out it comes. Then I need time to read it back, to make sure that what I've written meets my standards of evaluative feedback. In this regard, student work handed in and feedback given online has been a miracle, for what I now write is easy to read and I have the option of self-correcting with the delete button. Faster, more efficient, and infinitely neater. Even so, I continue to ask myself questions about the feedback I give:

- It is affirming?
- Is it respectful?
- Is it specific, rather than general?
- Does it reflect the clearly articulated performance criteria of the task?
- Does it make my judgment personal to me, rather than said as an authoritative truth?
- Does it point to areas of needed growth?
- Does it reflect my working hypothesis of the student's learning needs?
- Does it shift the locus of evaluation to the student?
- Is it clear, concise, and economical, rather than excessively wordy?
- Is it selective, rather than overwhelming the student by attempting to deal with every aspect of his or her performance that requires improvement?

So I read back, edit, and erase, here and there or I delete liberally if need be—to make sure I've said it just right. Does this take a long time? Of course. But this job is so important, with so much at stake, that the time I spend on it is well worth the cost. I take on writing evaluative comments as an essential part of my teaching load; it is as important as the acts of preparing and organizing my classes for instruction, as important as conducting an effective class discussion.

So what am I recommending? The suggestions that follow show the differences between evaluative comments that meet my various criteria and those that fail.

COMMENTS ABOUT EFFORT

- I can see much evidence of the effort you have put into this task.

    Rather than You are not trying.

- I know that this math work has been difficult for you.

    Rather than Your work in math is poor.

POINTING OUT SPECIFIC STRENGTHS

- I liked the way you used metaphor to create a mood.

    Rather than Good story.

- What I liked best about your drawing was the humor in it.

    Rather than A+ for your drawing.

POINTING OUT SPECIFIC WEAKNESSES

- Have another look, Philip, at those times 7 examples. You seem to be having some difficulty with them. Perhaps it would be helpful for you to revisit your times 7 tables? What do you think?

    Rather than You have 4 wrong out of 10.

- I see that the spelling is still a problem for you. I think I can help you. How 'bout coming to me for a conference?

    Rather than You are a terrible speller.

BEING CONCISE RATHER THAN OVERLY WORDY IN PROMOTING THINKING ABOUT SPECIFIC STRATEGIES

- You said that you think pollution is a problem. It would be helpful, I think, if you would give some examples of this. Your ideas become clearer when you can be more specific.

Rather than When I read your paper I saw that you seemed to be saying that pollution is a problem. I wonder what led you to that belief. Is this an assumption that you are making? You may be able to give some examples to support your opinion. What examples can you give?

PROVIDING CLEAR CRITERIA ABOUT THE EVALUATIVE STANDARDS

- In assessing your work, I'm using the following criteria to make my judgments: (1) your ability to formulate big ideas that have value and that lead to viable pupil inquiries; (2) your ability to develop a student inquiry that uses a higher order thinking operation as a lens to study data; and (3) your ability to create an inquiry that allows learners to study the big ideas.

SHIFTING THE LOCUS OF EVALUATION TO THE STUDENT

- From all the work you did this week, choose the 3 papers that you'd like to give me for my feedback to you.

  Rather than Turn in all your work for marking.

PROVIDING SUGGESTIONS FOR IMPROVEMENT

- It seems to me that the plans you have for building a birdhouse require a great deal of material. What size birdhouse did you have in mind? How about making a drawing to scale that will show how the birdhouse will look when it's finished?

  Rather than Your plans are not well worked out. You haven't thought this out! Start again, and this time, do a scale model.

CLEARLY FRAMED COMMENTS TO PARENTS

- Arlene is having difficulty with some of the tasks that require her to exercise thoughtful judgments. I'm helping her with activities that ask her to compare, observe, and classify data, and I'm beginning to see evidence of her growth. If you'd like to help at home, I think I can give you some ideas of how to do this.

Rather than Arlene is not working up to her potential.

In Figure 12.1, I've included two examples of how teachers' feedback can be affirming, be enabling, and provide suggestions for how a student may take the next steps in his or her learning.

WHAT'S IMPORTANT?

Some of my friends and colleagues have asked me why I would choose to invest so much time and energy into writing facilitative feedback on students' papers. Why would I not choose the easy way, when it seemed that "everyone else" was ticking off rights and wrongs and when, truthfully, there were so many other things I could be doing with my time. And especially when students themselves were initially aggravated by feedback that did not rank them by letters or numbers so that they "could know where they stood." Habituated to scales that ranked them, it took students a while to understand the value of evaluative comments and the uselessness of numbers and letters on their work in furthering their growth. So on many dimensions, the path was once again tortuous. Why go there?

A seventh-grade student once brought me a copy of her social studies test:

1. Queen Elizabeth died in _____.

2. William Shakespeare probably quit school in the year _____ to help his father.

3. The erection of the Globe Theatre took place in the year _____.

4. The three causes of the French Revolution were _____.

Figure 12.1. Examples of teacher feedback.

SALLY

Sally, a Grade 5 student, received this feedback from her teacher for her story, "The Dog Who Cried":

> Dear Sally,
>   I liked your story very much. I thought the idea about how the boy learned to take good care of his dog was very touching. I especially like the ending; you avoided the traditional cliché of everyone living "happily ever after" and left the reader in doubt. I thought that was very sophisticated. As you think about rewriting and editing, watch particularly the usage of *her and I* (the pronoun *her* being in the objective case) for *she and I*, and for split infinitives (e.g., to speak thoughtfully, rather than to thoughtfully speak). Let me know if I can be of help in your rewrite. I think you have a real talent for writing and I'm looking forward to seeing more of your stories.

TODD

Todd, a Grade 3 boy who'd handed in an arithmetic paper reading

$$6 + 3 = 9$$
$$4 + 5 = 10$$
$$7 + 3 = 10$$
$$5 + 6 = 12$$
$$3 + 4 = 7$$
$$8 + 3 = 12$$

received this feedback from his teacher:

> Dear Todd:
>   If 4 + 4 add up to 8, what do you make of 4 + 5? Can you check this on your paper?
>   If 6 + 6 add up to 12, what do you make of 5 + 6? Can you check this too?
>   I noted that your sum for 8 + 3 was 12. Marlene said 8 + 3 = 10. Who is correct? What do you think?
>   Let me know how you figure this out.

5. The Renaissance depended upon

   _____.

6. In what year were metals first discovered? _____

7. What are the two main periods in the Age of Metals?

   _____

8. What are the four main divisions of the human race?

   _____

I asked myself a question that a student had taught me to ask about the choices a teacher makes: What's important? I looked at the test and, by the nature and focus of the questions posed in this test, I saw what was important to this teacher and what this teacher was teaching her students. And I knew that the sum of it is not only worthless, but also implicitly teaching all the wrong messages about learning, about school, about the big ideas of history. I knew that the sum total of such evaluative practices are, in the long run, a deterrent to developing an informed citizenry. And I felt an overwhelming sense of waste and loss.

Goodlad, Soder, and Sirotnik's book *The Moral Dimensions of Teaching* (1990) has reminded me that "teaching is a moral act." Every action carried out by teachers is based on that teacher having made a moral choice about what's important. I've come to learn and understand what's important for me; I've come to understand better the reasons for my choices and actions, and I am clear that this is what I want to do and this is who I want to be. And as they say, "There's no free lunch." So choices come with prices—and the prices are time investment in the work and the tough uphill road of teaching my students and their parents, "what's important?" But whoever said teaching was supposed to be easy?

⑬

"4 Imprtint Things for Noo Teechrs to 'Member"

THERE WAS an e-mail message this morning from a longtime friend and colleague at the university, Stan Kanehara, the administrative assistant to the dean. "Stan the Man" has been one of the strongest supporters of my work, and his assistance over the years has been nothing short of fundamental to my teaching and administrative endeavors. The message contained an article from the *Toronto Globe and Mail,* Canada's premier newspaper, announcing the reconsideration of the mandatory retirement law for the Canadian professoriate. Too late for me. But it did give me pause to reflect whether, given the chance, I might pick up Julie's wood sculpture and plant it anew in yet another faculty office? Or have I by now cut the ties that bound me to a regular teaching job, happy in having my options open to working with teachers and students "on call"?

Truth be told, I have begun a new life, filled with writing, and I am content to be creatively involved in developing multimedia software for students at all classroom levels. (Yes, Mildred. There is life after retirement.) I am content to respond to invitations to do workshops whenever they arrive and to enjoy brief moments of being with teachers and children again. I no longer yearn for the teacher's life—the thrills, frustrations, challenges, and excitement that filled my days for so many years. But it was not an easy transition, and I confess that when I do come into a school, the smell of chalk and sweaty running shoes still evokes a nostalgia that touches my heart.

So now, at the end of my story about my professional journey, I want to wind up by writing some parting words to new teachers, especially those who are facing beginnings not unlike mine.

WORDS OF CAUTION: STEPPING GINGERLY INTO THE WORLD OF UNCERTAINTY

So many beginning teachers have asked me over the years, "How do I do *this*?" or "How do I deal with this behavior?" or other variations on the theme of "Tell me what I should do." For surely, the problems faced by all teachers, whether they are new to the profession or veterans, are complex and pervasive; and it is a given that we all, at different points of our teaching lives, seek help from those who are more experienced, to "fix" what is "broken."

But nettlesome dilemmas are the stuff of daily life in classrooms. Pure fantasy is perfect classrooms in which all students are sweet, complaint, and eager to learn; where they sit quietly and calmly; where teachers teach with authority and children obey and do as they are told. The truth is that the best, most exciting, most teaching-rich classrooms are precisely those in which things go wrong and where crises arise from moment to moment and the course of the day is uneven, eventful, sometimes turbulent, and only rarely calm. Given the real world of teaching, the best that we teachers can hope for is to possess the tools that will allow us to perceive dilemmas with intelligence and sensitivity and to make thoughtful, informed decisions that guide teaching actions. I guess this is like saying that each of us needs to find ways to strengthen our personal power to perceive and to act with intelligence and wisdom—to do what we think is right and to have confidence in what we do. This, regrettably, doesn't come at the point of entering the profession, but they are goals seriously worth dedicating one's professional life to.

As anyone who has spent a day in a classroom will know, there are problems that defy "fixing." In such cases, we do the best we can; we put Band-Aids on cancerous wounds and give succor, in the absence of a magic pill. But I have learned never to underestimate doing the best that I can do and accepting the limitations under which I can act. If all I can do is give a desperately unhappy child a single good year, that is a worthwhile endeavor.

Using knowledge to make meaning of what I see happening, using my ability to make decisions that are appropriate to the meanings being made, to trust myself to take the risks of action, to make judgments about the effectiveness of decisions—these are tools worth having and that make a difference to who I am and what I can accomplish. With such tools, teachers grow in the awareness that while there are no easy, clear-cut answers in teaching, there are decisions that we make; that in the presence of confusing and ambiguous issues, we search for appropriate courses of action, rather than resolutions; that decisions are for better or for worse; that even in the best of times, we choose from among several less-than-good alternatives; and that many of life's problems cannot be solved. Learning not to reproach oneself for not being able to fix everything and solve all problems is probably the key to staying the course.

Yet having said all that, I recognize once again, from my own beginnings and from the many teachers with whom I've worked over the years, that those first teaching days are filled with anxiety, with the desperate need to know with certainty the "answers" to all the complex, riveting, world-shaking questions that confound all teachers every day of their teaching lives. I recognize the sense of safety we get from believing that there *are* answers. And, of course, I am aware of the tension in having to assess situations, make judgments, and take appropriate action. If we could all know with certainty *everything* about teaching, life in classrooms would be so simple. But for anyone looking for the simple, teaching is not the answer.

The need for certainty, for the security that closure brings, seems to be a built-in feature of our human make-up. The human organism needs to resolve ambiguity. When closure can be reached, it is accompanied by a palpable physical relief—a sort of physiological sigh. Having answers for all the problems in teaching makes for a secure feeling. Not knowing for certain, having to interpret each classroom event, trying to understand what is going on, making informed judgments, and risking action provoke anxiety.

Make no mistake about it. It feels good to know the answers. It is stressful to have to take the risks involved in applying knowledge to practice, where answers are rarely clear, where the meaning we make is our own, and where the best answer often is "It depends." Even experienced teachers who acknowledge ambiguity and operate with a higher tolerance for it often wish for the relief that clear answers would bring. Especially for beginning teachers, who suffer from insecurities associated with their lack of experience, answers appear to reduce the stress of teaching. We look to our teachers, to workshops, and to books to tell us; and in the end, we are usually left to our own resources. The beginning teacher is never certain of his or her competence. Nor has the stress of uncertainty about action been reduced. Crossing the bridge between knowing and applying that knowledge to action is the heart of the professional journey. If you think you learn all about that in less than a lifetime in the classroom, you are going to be in for a big surprise.

Knowledge alone is far from a guarantee that a person will behave wisely. We all know that we should eat healthy food, exercise regularly, stop smoking, give more time to our primary relationships, stop working so hard. But action involves knowing how. It implies the need to examine what we have done, to make thoughtful assessments so that we may learn from the action and take the next appropriate steps. It incorporates elements of risk, since even wise action may produce less-than-desirable results. It is no wonder that action is fraught with uncertainty. It is no wonder that teachers, and especially beginning teachers, wish to remain safe in those security-giving domains of certainty that pure knowledge brings.

The best you can do at the starting post is to take on the challenge of stepping gingerly into the uncertain world of meaning making, where you are on your own, trying to apply what you know, in the process of choosing how to act in response to the hundreds of dilemmas that make up a teacher's day.

ADVICE TO "NOO TEECHRS"

If I could have had a mentor to give me some words of advice as I entered my first classroom, what would I have liked to have heard?

A reminder from Hippocrates: First, do no harm. All children should feel better, more capable, at the end of the school day than they did at the beginning. If they feel worse, less able, then their school experience has hurt them rather than helped them. No matter what you do, no matter how you bungle, how ineptly you carry out your lesson in grammar, first, do no harm.

A reminder that learning to teach is a lifelong process. If you are looking for the miracle, the magic bullet that will allow you to "change your stuff" and zip from student to expert teacher at the stroke of the graduation bell, you are going to be seriously disappointed. Learning from mistakes, from blunders, from gaffes, is what teaches us the important steps in the process. Beating yourself up for not being expert is a quick road to burn out. I call on my grandson's advice here for those who are unable to accept their fallibilities: Gwive yourself a break.

A reminder to be certain, absolutely certain, that teaching is what you want to do. If you are not getting satisfaction and joy from working with students, then find something different. Life is too short to remain in a job, no matter how secure tenure is, that is ultimately too stressful or too unsatisfying. The pain will defeat you, and it will leak out onto the children. The counterpart of that is, enjoy the students. If you are not finding pleasure in being with them, it's time to move on.

The last word belongs to Eli, who wrote in his best, 5-year-old printing, his advice to new teachers.

4 Imprtint Things for Noo Teechrs to Member

1. Sumtims ther are no rite ansers.
2. Its eezier with a buddy.
3. Alwees smile.
4. Whan yor braen gets hevy be sher to empte sum and thn play and get sum rest.

EPILOGUE

I'm taking the early morning flight to Chicago, and as the plane is boarding, I'm still grouchy from a 5:30 a.m. wake-up call, a restless night, long lines at the airport, and a dour-faced U.S. Immigration officer, who looks at my U.S. passport and studies my face as if I might be John Dillinger in drag. I'm relieved to settle myself into the aisle seat, take care to buckle my seatbelt, and put my book into the pocket of the seat in front of me. I settle back with a final glance out the window to the mountains of Vancouver, still covered with winter snow, although it is far into the spring. The man in the window seat smiles, and soon we begin to chat.

"What do you do?" he asks me.

"I'm a teacher," I tell him, with a pride of purpose and position that has never left me. That I can still feel it, after all these years, makes me feel incredibly blessed. This teaching life has been well worth living.

References

Adam, M., Chambers, R., Fukui, S., Gluska, J., & Wassermann, S. (1991). *Evaluation practices for the graduation program*. Victoria, BC, Canada: Ministry of Education.

Adler, R. B., & Towne, N. (2002). *Looking out, looking in*. Belmont, CA: Wadsworth.

Ashton-Warner, S. (1959). *Spinster*. New York: Simon & Schuster.

Ashton-Warner, S. (1963). *Teacher*. New York: Simon & Schuster.

Ashton-Warner, S. (1972). *Spearpoint*. New York: Knopf.

Ashton-Warner, S. (1979). *I passed this way*. New York: Knopf.

Ayers, W. (2004). *On the side of the child: Summerhill revisited*. New York: Teachers College Press.

Bickerton, L., Chambers, R., Dart, G., Fukui, S., Gluska, J., McNeill, B., et al. (1991). *Cases for teaching in the secondary school*. Coquitlam, BC, Canada: CaseWorks.

Bloom, B. (Ed.). (1956). *Taxonomy of educational objectives. Handbook I: Cognitive domain*. New York: David McKay.

Bracey, G. W. (1998, December). Minds of our own. *Phi Delta Kappan, 80*(4), 328–329.

Brammer, L. M. (1993). *The helping relationship: Process and skills* (5th ed.). Boston: Allyn & Bacon.

Carbo, M. (1997). *What every principal should know about teaching reading*. Syosset, NY: National Reading Styles Institute.

Carkhuff, R. (1969). *Helping and human relations*. New York: Holt Rinehart.

Carkhuff, R., & Berenson, B. (1976). *Teaching as treatment*. Amherst, MA: Human Resources Development Press.

Carkhuff, R., & Truax, C. (1967). *Toward effective counseling and psychotherapy*. Chicago: Aldine.

Ewing, D. (1991). *Inside the Harvard Business School*. New York: Times Books.

Fadiman, D. (1992). *Why do these children love school?* Santa Monica, CA: Pyramid Film & Video.

Featherstone, J. (1971). *Schools where children learn*. New York: Liveright.

Feldman, R. S. (2002). *Development across the life span* (3rd ed.). Englewood, NJ: Prentice Hall.

Feynman, R. (1985). *Surely you're joking, Mr. Feynman*. New York: Norton.

Flanders, N. (1970). *Interaction analysis system*. Ann Arbor: University of Michigan Press.

Gamoran, A., Anderson, C., Quiroz, P., Secada, W., Williams, T., & Ashmann, S. (2003). *Transforming teaching in math and science*. New York: Teachers College Press.

Gazda, G., Asbury, F., Balzer, F., & Childers, W. (1991). *Human relations development* (4th ed.). New York: Pearson, Allyn & Bacon.

Goodlad, J., Soder, R., & Sirotnik, K. (1990). *The moral dimensions of teaching*. San Francisco: Jossey-Bass.

Hamachek, D. E. (1997). *Encounters with others*. London: International Thomson Publishing.

Harris, T. (1967). *I'm OK, you're OK*. New York: Avon Books.

Harwell, J. M. (2002). *Complete learning disabilities handbook*. San Francisco: Jossey-Bass.

Henry, J. (1963). *Culture against man*. New York: Random House.

Hole, S., & McEntee, G. (2003). Reflection is at the heart of practice. In G. McEntee, J. Appleby, J. Dowd, J. Grant, S. Hole, & P. Silva, *At the heart of teaching: A guide to reflective practice* (pp. 50–60). New York: Teachers College Press.

Hood, L. (1988). *Sylvia! The biography of Sylvia Ashton-Warner*. London: Viking.

Kamii, C. (1991). *Early literacy: A constructivist foundation for whole language*. Washington, DC: National Education Association.

Lerner, J. (1993). *Learning disabilities: Theories, diagnosis, and teaching strategies* (6th ed.). Boston: Houghton Mifflin.

Lindner, R. (1954). *The fifty-minute hour*. New York: Delta.

Marshall, J. (2003, November). Math wars: Taking sides. *Phi Delta Kappan, 85*(3), 193–200.

McEntee, G., Appleby, J., Dowd, J., Grant, J., Hole, S., & Silva, P. (2003). *At the heart of teaching: A guide to reflective practice*. New York: Teachers College Press.

McIntyre, E. (Ed). (1996). *Balanced instruction: Strategies and skills in whole language*. Norwood, MA: Christopher-Gordon.

Mercer, C. D., & Mercer, A. (2000). *Teaching students with learning problems* (6th ed.) Englewood, NJ: Prentice Hall.

Moursund, J. (1993). *The process of counseling and therapy*. Englewood Cliffs, NJ: Prentice Hall.

Neill, A. S. (1960). *Summerhill*. New York: Hart.

Parsons, T. (1971). *Guided self-analysis*. Unpublished manuscript, University of California–Berkeley.

Perls, F. (1969). *In and out the garbage pail*. New York: Bantam.

Purkey, W. (1970). *Self-concept and school achievement*. Englewood, NJ: Prentice Hall.

Raines, S. C. (1995). *Whole language across the curriculum*. New York: Teachers College Press.

Raths, L. (1998). *Meeting the needs of children: Creating trust and security*. Troy, NY: Educator's International Press.

Raths, L., Harmin, M., & Simon, S. (1978). *Values and teaching* (2nd ed.). Columbus, OH: Charles Merrill.

Raths, L., Wassermann, S., Jonas, A., & Rothstein, A. (1966). *Teaching for thinking: Theory and application*. Columbus, OH: Charles Merrill.

Raths, L., Wassermann, S., Jonas, A., & Rothstein, A. (1986). *Teaching for thinking: Theory, strategies, and activities for the classroom* (2nd ed.). New York: Teachers College Press.

Rogers, C. (1961). *On becoming a person*. Boston: Houghton Mifflin.

Rogers, C. (1969). *Freedom to learn*. Columbus, OH: Charles Merrill.

Rosmarin, A. (1985). The art of leading a discussion. *On Teaching and Learning, 1,* 34–39.

Roswell, F., & Chall, J. (1976). *Roswell-Chall Diagnostic Reading Test*. New York: Essay Press.

Schön, D. (1983). *The reflective practitioner*. New York: Basic Books.

Silberman, C. (1970). *Crisis in the classroom*. New York: Random House.

Snygg, D. (1966). Cognitive field theory of learning. In W. Waetjen & R. Leeper, (Eds.), *Learning and mental health in the schools* (pp. 77–96). Alexandria, VA: Association of Supervision and Curriculum Development.

Taba, H., & Levine, S. (1963). *Thinking in elementary school children*. Cooperative Research Project No. 1574, U.S. Office of Education, San Francisco: San Francisco State College.

Thomas, L. (1983). *The youngest science: Notes of a medicine watcher*. New York: Viking.

Veatch, J. (1966). *Reading in the elementary school*. New York: Ronald Press.

Wassermann, S. (1976, November). Organic teaching in the primary classroom. *Phi Delta Kappan, 58*(3), 264–268.

Wassermann, S. (1986). Beliefs and personal power: The difference between a chairperson and a charperson is how she behaves. *College Teaching, 34* (2), 69–74.

Wassermann, S. (1991). What's evaluation for? *Childhood Education, 68,* 93–96.

Wassermann, S. (1993). "He's driving me crazy!" In S. Wassermann, *Getting down to cases* (pp. 95–101). New York: Teachers College Press.

Wassermann, S. (2000). *Serious players in the primary classroom* (2nd ed.). New York: Teachers College Press.

Wassermann, S., & Eggert, W. (1976). Profiles of teaching competency. *Canadian Journal of Education, 1*(1), 67–93.

Wassermann, S., & Ivany, J. W. G. (1996). *The new teaching elementary science: Who's afraid of spiders?* (2nd ed.). New York: Teachers College Press.

Index

About the Author

S ELMA WASSERMANN is Professor Emerita in the Faculty of education at Simon Fraser University, Vancouver, Canada. She has taught in elementary schools in New York and California, as well as at Newark State College and Hofstra University. She holds an EdD from New York University. A recipient of the University Excellence in Teaching Award, she has published widely, including five Teachers College Press books: *Serious Players in the Primary Classroom: Empowering Children through Active Learning Experiences*; *The New Teaching Elementary Science: Who's Afraid of Spiders?* (with George Ivany); *Teaching for Thinking: Theory, Strategies and Activities for the Classroom*, second edition (with Louis E. Raths, Arthur Jonas, and Arnold Rothstein); *Getting Down to Cases*; and *Introduction to Case Method Teaching—A Guide to the Galaxy*. She lives in Vancouver with her husband, Jack, and cat, Mischa.